GIRL WITH A PLAN

SUCCESS STRATEGIES FOR LIFE AND BUSINESS

Maria Kritikos

FOUNDER OF THE LADIES WHO LUNCH® NETWORK AND CREATOR OF THE THE SHE'S IN BIZ BLUEPRINT

Ladies WHO Lunch® Network Ltd.

VANCOUVER, BRITISH COLUMBIA

Copyright © 2018 by **Maria Kritikos**

All rights reserved. No part of this publication may be reproduced, distributed or transmitted in any form or by any means, without prior written permission.

Maria Kritikos/Ladies WHO Lunch ® Network Ltd
Vancouver, British Columbia
www.GirlWithAPlanBook.com

Girl With A Plan/ Maria Kritikos. -- 1st ed.
ISBN 978-1-7753001-0-6

For my sister Joanna whose relentless support and encouragement urged me to pursue this passion of mine and bring it to life.

For Mom and Dad

For my best friend and light of my life, my son Andrew.

For all the women in the Ladies WHO Lunch® Network

"I COME AS ONE, BUT I STAND AS 10,000."
MAYA ANGELOU

A *dream* written down with a date becomes a *goal*.

A *goal* broken down into steps becomes a *plan*.

A *plan* backed by action becomes a **reality**.

CHAPTERS

INTRODUCTION 8

THE END IS THE BEGINNING 16
LIVING OUT OF A SUITCASE 20
BE A GOAL GETTER 22
DECIDE WHAT YOU WANT 28
I CAN AND I WILL. WATCH ME. 32
BE YOUR OWN HERO 34
WHO ARE YOU? 36
WHAT DO YOU STAND FOR? 42
WHAT DO YOU EXPECT? 48
BE UNREASONABLE 55
WHAT'S IT GOING TO TAKE 61
THE ONLY DIFFERENCE 64
BRAINWASH YOURSELF 72
THE VOICE IN YOUR HEAD 80
SAY GOODBYE TO NEGATIVE NELLY 88
THE EVICTION NOTICE 94
DON'T BE A ZOMBIE 97
TUNNEL VISION 100
IMPOSSIBLE TO FAIL 106
ATTITUDE VS. IQ 110
GETTING TO KNOW YOU 115

BRING IT TO THE TOP AND LET IT GO 119
COMPETITION IS FOR COPYCATS 121
THE POWER IS IN THE RESPONSE 127
SQUARE PEGS DON'T FIT IN ROUND HOLES 130
FALL DOWN SEVEN, GET UP EIGHT 135
INTERESTED VS. COMMITTED 137
YOU ARE THE PROBLEM AND THE SOLUTION 143
THIS IS THE LAW 149
WATCH YOUR WORDS 155
START BEFOR YOU'RE READY 161
FEAR IS A BAD MAN 164
GET ON IT GIRL 168
MOTIVATION IS A LIAR 176
SAY NO TO MAKE ROOM FOR YES 180
HOW TO STAY FOCUSED 182
SHINY OBJECT SYNDROME 186
CHASING RABBITS 192
IS IT A DMA OR A TW? 198
ENERGY VAMPIRES 202
THE POWER OF ASSOCIATION 204
MONKEY SEE, MONKEY DO 210
THE PROBLEM IS WE THINK WE HAVE TIME 214
IT'S JUST A HABIT 216
GO TO A PLACE OF DISCOMFORT 218
GET OUT OF TOWN 222
DRESS FOR SUCCESS 226
BEES LOVE HONEY 230

THE LAST 5 MINUTES	232
IT ALL ADDS UP	236
DON' TAKE THE NEXT FLIGHT OUT	239
KEEP IT MOVING SISTER!	242

INTRODUCTION

"THE MOMENT YOU CLAIM RESPONSIBILITY FOR YOUR LIFE IS THE MOMENT YOU HAVE THE POWER TO CHANGE IT."

What if I told you, that you could have ANYTHING you've ever wanted in your life? Anything you've dreamed possible, anything you've imagined, you CAN have it.

What if I told you there was only ONE person that could make that happen? Would you want to know who that is?

Well, guess what! You look at that person in the mirror every day - that person is YOU.

If I could tell you the two things that are stopping you from living your dream life right now, would you want to know what they are?

I bet that's one of the reasons you're reading this book isn't it?

Are you ready?

The two culprits that are getting in the way of your dream life are FEAR and YOU. When I say you, I mean the limiting beliefs you have about yourself, and what you think you can and cannot do.

If I were to ask you why you're not living the life you want, your answer will most likely have two dreaded "B" words in it. Those words are BECAUSE and BUT. My response will also have only two words WHY NOT?

You'll answer with another B word, "because", and you'll give me all the reasons why you're not living your dream.

Whatever comes after one of those "B" words is your limiting belief. All the reasons why you think you can't do or have something define your limiting beliefs. We all have them. The difference with successful people is they identify what they are, and they move past them. They know limiting beliefs aren't true.

What kind of fears am I talking about? You know, the usual ones. I'm talking about fear of being laughed at because your idea is silly, fear of failure, fear of not being smart enough, good enough, educated enough, or "fill in the blank" enough.

You may not be living your dream because you feel don't have the right resources at your disposal. Or, because you feel you don't know HOW. Maybe you believe the ones that are living their dream are somehow smarter than you, have more money, more training, a better team, more time, and whatever other excuse you've been telling yourself up until now.

You picked up this book for a reason. It's my mission to help you kick all of your limiting beliefs to the curb! Tell them goodbye. Tell them to shut up, and to go away!

Now that I've introduced you to the person that will make this happen, what if I told you there is a way to achieve anything you've ever dreamed of, would you want to know HOW? On my personal journey, full of many twists and turns I discovered the secret to success. The secret to living a life I dreamed of. I'm about to share everything I learned with you.

The Ladies WHO Lunch® Network is a global inspirational networking group for female entrepreneurs. I started it with nothing but a Facebook page, and a tiny, rusty beat-up computer, all from my humble kitchen table, which served as both my eating area and my home office!

I had no business plan, no money, no resources, no team, and absolutely NO IDEA how I was going to make this network come alive. Not only did it come alive, it would thrive and continue to grow into the global community that it is today.

I did know one thing. I knew I was determined to figure it out. I was determined to find a way when there was none. I want to show you how you can do the same.

"ALL DAYDREAMS AND WISHES BECOME REALITIES IF WE KEEP THEM CONSTANTLY BEFORE US - PUT FEAR BEHIND - PUSH AWAY ALL RESERVATIONS, IFS, ANDS AND BUTS."

It starts with a dream and then a PLAN.

My life today is nothing like it was 10 years ago, nor is it the same as it was a year ago. I am certain that it will look different yet again next year. Life is funny like that, what you think will stay the same forever often gets away from you. Often the worst experiences of our lives turn out to be our biggest blessings and our greatest teachers.

"OUR GREATEST GIFTS COME WRAPPED IN SAND PAPER AND THORNS, WE JUST DON'T SEE IT THAT WAY AT THE TIME."- LISA NICHOLS

I went from being a reserved girl in high school who experienced a very sheltered upbringing, to marrying into a very prominent and influential family. I lived a very comfortable, some would say fairy tale like existence, until I unexpectedly found myself a single mom of a 2 year old, homeless, and sleeping on my mom's couch.

Let me tell you. Life can throw you a curve ball at any time. The difference now is that I'm ready for it. And, it all boils down to how you react to your circumstances, and the actions you take.

We all have a choice at any given moment. It's how we react in those moments of choice, and the decisions we make, that will shape our lives and create our future.

You are not your circumstances. You do have the power and the capability to rise above them. I wrote this book to show you how. To help you realize that YOU are the only one holding you back from living the life you dream of. Not only that, but to realize it's your responsibility to create your happiness along with your financial success. NOBODY ELSE'S! Once you get this and understand it, you become unstoppable.

I created the Ladies WHO Lunch® Network to show women how truly powerful they are, as individuals, and as a collective.

Taking action in spite of fear, doubt, hesitation and all of the untruths that your mind will feed you is the key making progress.

My goal is to inspire you to realize your passion and to help you live it. I trust this book will be a tool to guide you, and will help set you on the path to the freedom and happiness you deserve.

This book will teach you what it means to have a winning mindset that serves as the foundation where all dreams become possible.

I share my key insights, tips and best strategies to help you develop this foundation. You can read this book in order, or you can go from chapter to chapter. The only thing I ask is that you take action with what you learn. If you use one key insight to help transform your life, then my mission with writing this book is complete.

Read these insights over and over. Pass it on to a friend who you know will benefit from the words on these pages. Repetition is one of the keys to success. One of my favourite expressions is: I'd rather read one book a thousand times than 1,000 books one time.

WHO IS THE GIRL WITH A PLAN?

- She is tenacious in the face of adversity.
- When she falls, she gets right back up.
- She takes action in spite of fear.
- She is intentional about the life she wants to live.
- She wants to make a difference.
- Her choices reflect her values.
- She desires to make an impact in the world.
- She knows that mistakes are just lessons.
- She is not afraid of failure.
- She has clear goals.
- She knows she can HAVE, BE or DO anything she wants.
- She knows she has the power to create whatever life she dreams of.

- She takes 100% responsibility for her life, goals and dreams.

- She lives her life ON PURPOSE.

- She always has options and chooses freely.

- She focuses on the SOLUTION not the PROBLEM.

- She surrounds herself with inspiring, supportive individuals.

- She knows that anything is possible.

- She lives each day with passion.

- She is committed to her success.

- She believes in herself.

- She dreams BIG.

- The Girl With A Plan is powerful and unstoppable.

- She is FREE.

- She is INDEPENDENT.

- She is AUTHENTIC.

SHE IS A GIRL WITH A PLAN

> *Sometimes our greatest gifts come wrapped in sandpaper and thorns.*
>
> — LISA NICHOLS

#GirlWithAPlanBook

CHAPTER 1

THE END IS THE BEGINNING

"WHEN GOD GIVES YOU A NEW BEGINNING, IT STARTS WITH AN ENDING. BE THANKFUL FOR CLOSED DOORS. THEY OFTEN GUIDE US TO THE RIGHT ONE."

I didn't know it at the time but the end of my life as I knew it was in fact a wonderful new beginning. You would have a hard time convincing me of that then. My whole world had crumbled, snatched away from me all in the blink of an eye. It was as though the rug had been pulled out from under me. I fell fast and hard.

At 36 years old, after five years of marriage, my husband announced that he was moving out, leaving me bewildered and alone with our 2-year-old son, just five days before Christmas. Shock and disbelief were the best terms to describe my immediate feelings and reaction. Then came the incredible anger, which would turn to disbelief again before the unthinkable journey of trying to make sense of something that I did NOT understand.

Why was this happening to me? How could he do this to me? And how did I not see it coming? The next year and a half was a surreal feeling. Living in a house that was once occupied by a family, with one piece now missing. I remember losing 8 pounds the week my husband left and not being able to eat a thing.

I went from living in a 5,000 square foot home with a full time live in nanny, driving fancy cars and being financially "secure" (whatever I thought that meant at the time), to having to sell the house and move into my parents' two bedroom apartment taking up residence on their couch.

All I heard from my family was you can't make it on your own, you need help, we need to buy a bigger place together so you can survive. You won't be able to make it as a single mom. It's not possible.

I knew they meant well, and only wanted to support me the best way they knew how, but there was a fire in my belly that couldn't be put out, and a belief that I COULD make it on my own, despite the odds and despite my circumstances.

I remember doing a real estate deal that resulted in a big commission cheque at the time. This commission helped me put a down payment on a small condo for my son and I. This was the beginning of my new life. A complete 180° from the life I had known before. The change was hard for me to deal with for many years. I harboured a lot of anger and resentment. I had a victim mentality and truly held on to the fact that my life would never be the same again. I never considered that perhaps it could be better. That was not a possibility I had the capacity to consider. The words positive mindset were not a part of my vocabulary during that experience.

These feelings dissipated with time particularly after I attended a weekend seminar and learned that we are the creators of our own life. This was in November of 2012.

It was this ULTIMATE realization for me and it was the belief and epiphany, I WAS THE ONE IN CHARGE of my happiness. This was MY job, not anyone else's. That was the game changer for me.

"And once the storm is over you won't remember how you made it through, how you managed to survive. You won't even be sure in fact, whether the storm is really over. But one thing is certain. When you come out of the storm you won't be the same person who walked in." – Haruki Murakami

This was a catalyst for me. After the weekend seminar, my life was never the same. It set me off on a journey that inspired me to create the Ladies WHO Lunch® Network and change my life forever.

If you're reading this, know that I'm speaking directly to YOU. I encourage you to take a risk, to dream and to dream big, and not let fear dictate your life. As the expression goes - everything you've ever wanted IS on the other side of fear. I know you may feel scared, but I want you to do it scared anyways.

One of the greatest regrets of the dying was that they were not confident enough to go after what they really wanted in life, they listened to other people whose voices rang louder than their own and in the end they were filled with regrets. Don't let that be you, don't get to the end and wish you had.

I believe I went through these life altering events which led me to the ah-ha moment of living my life, my way, and realizing it can be everything I dream of, so that you can create that same realization in your life too.

These chapters are guides to living life by your own design. Carry them with you everywhere. Keep this book in your purse. Read it in the line up at Starbucks, while you're waiting at the doctor's office, or picking your children up from school.

I trust that after you finish reading Girl With A Plan and intentionally implement what resonates for you, you will be one step closer to reaching your goals.

Enjoy!

CHAPTER 2

LIVING OUT OF A SUITCASE

We never really know where the road of life will take us. What we do know is that we have the power to adapt to any situation that we encounter, as long as we keep in the right mindset.

What followed the divorce was to date one of the hardest times that I've had to experience. It was a riches to rags story. I went from living in a mansion, to having no place to call a home of my own. Living out of my suitcase, sleeping on my mom's couch, and caring full time for my two-year-old son. Without a doubt, I can now say that if I didn't go through this, I would not be where I am today.

Trials and tribulations teach us strength, resilience and determination. They also teach us to appreciate the times when things are going well. I believe that the most successful people

Everyone you look up to has fallen down more times than you have tried to get up.

are those that have gone through difficult times and have emerged triumphant and victorious. They are those who have endured and hung on long after others would have let go.

There's a certain grit and perseverance that those who have lost it all feel. I promised myself that when I became strong again, I would never allow myself to be in this situation again. And that's when I resolved to be the creator of my own life, and to live life on my terms, how I wanted. I never wanted to place my life under anyone else's control ever again. Not for my happiness or my financial destiny.

"When you create your own happiness and financial destiny an incredible thing happens, nobody can ever take it away from you."

CHAPTER 3

BE A GOAL GETTER

From very early on, I've always been obsessed with goal setting. In high school my quote in the yearbook was "Obstacles are what you see when you take your eyes off the goal". Over the years, I've made it my mission to understand what it takes to be successful in life and in business. I've always wondered WHY some people have everything they've ever wanted, and why some just keep dreaming about it but it never arrives?

This question kept me up at night. So, I made it my mission to discover what the secret to this success was. What did these people know that I didn't? I HAD to find out. I needed to know these secrets so I could start implementing these strategies and change my life!

I read books upon books on the subject and studied the success of others. And, you know what I found out? They all spoke the same language. They all read the same books and used the same phrases and acted in a certain way.

Wow. I thought, how come everyone doesn't know this and do it? They certainly would achieve everything they've ever wanted if only they followed these simple principles.

Obstacles are what you see when you take your eyes off your goal.

I used to teach high school. Teaching is in my blood. I'm most passionate about sharing my knowledge with others.

When I created my secret formula for success I knew I wanted to share it with you. I use it and have applied it consistently in my life to get the results I crave and you can do this too!

These are the **6 Principles To Success** that I implement everyday.

THE 1ST IS **PERSEVERANCE**.

A commitment to hang in there and push through until you get the result that you desire.

THE 2ND IS **PATIENCE**.

Allowing the universe to bring you what you desire at the right time and TRUSTING IN THE PROCESS.

THE 3RD IS **COMMITMENT**.

A promise to yourself that you'll stick with the program until you see results. Not when you feel like it, but all the time, even when you'd rather be doing something else. A commitment is doing something no matter what.

THE 4TH IS **CONSISTENT ACTION**.

The highest achievers are ALL action takers! Every single one of them, they make decisions and they act quickly and implement at a ridiculously fast rate. They are not afraid of failing. In fact they welcome failures and re-name them opportunities for growth and chances to do better or different next time.

THE 5TH IS **BELIEF**.

A solid and firm belief in yourself that what you are trying to accomplish IS possible and that you CAN make it happen.

THE 6TH IS **ACCOUNTABILITY**.

We all need someone to hold us accountable to what we say we are going to do. Once you declare your intention to another person, it no longer lives inside you and now someone is a witness to your actions. You don't want to let them down.

Throughout the book you will learn many examples of each of these 6 principles in action.

A goal without a plan is just a wish.
ANTOINE DE SAINT-EXUPÉRY

HOW TO BE AN EFFECTIVE GOAL GETTER

Ever since I can remember I've been obsessed with goals. Obsessed with setting them and finding out what is the best way to achieve them. I've probably read every book under the sun about goal setting, but my favourite mentor on this subject is Brian Tracy. He is clear, precise and easy to understand, and I recommend every single one of his books. My favourite book of his being, "Eat That Frog".

There have been numerous studies on goal setting but the one that comes to mind and is most often used is a study done by Harvard University:

So, Why Do 3% of Harvard MBAs Make Ten Times as Much as the Other 97% Combined?

The answer is a simple: They set clear, written goals for the future and make plans to accomplish them.

In 1979, interviewers asked new graduates from the Harvard's MBA Program and found that:

84% had no specific goals at all
13% had goals but they were not committed to paper
3% had clear, written goals and plans to accomplish them

In 1989, the interviewers again interviewed the graduates of that class. You can guess the results. The 13% of the class who had goals were earning, on average, twice as much as the 84 percent who had no goals at all. Even more staggering

– the three percent who had clear, written goals were earning, on average, ten times as much as the other 97 percent put together!

I've always been a huge fan of writing goals down on paper. It's not enough to have them floating around in your head. You need to see them and look at them EVERY DAY.

Here are my tips for goal setting:

1. Write your monthly goals on a plain white sheet of paper and tape it to the fridge. I do this every month, then look back and become astonished at what I have accomplished. The timing may not always be what you want, but that doesn't matter. As Brian Tracy says, there are no unrealistic goals, only unrealistic deadlines. So if you haven't achieved the goal by the time you anticipated, simply adjust your timing.

2. Write your goals on cue cards and carry them with you everywhere. Look at them throughout the day. Or, look at them once in the morning and once before you sleep.

3. Write your goals daily in a notebook. Write your goals each day without looking back at yesterday's goals.

4. Always write your goals in the present tense: I have, I am...

5. Repetition, repetition, repetition. Keep repeating your goals over and over until they are engrained into your subconscious mind and until you believe them to be true.

Before we can achieve our goals we have to know what we want. We need to get clear. This might sound simple, but so many people tell me what they don't want, as opposed to what they do want.

The #1 reason successful people get more work done faster is that they are absolutely clear about their goals and objectives. They don't deviate from them.

Do you know what the major reason for procrastination and lack of motivation is? It's vagueness and confusion about what you're trying to do. So the greater clarity you have the faster you will reach your goals and the more productive you will become.

Only about 3 percent of adults have clear written goals. It is these people who accomplish 5 and 10 times more than those who do not take the time to write out exactly what they want!

CHAPTER 4

DECIDE WHAT YOU WANT

What do you want?

You'd be surprised at how many times I ask this question and the result is a blank face looking back at me.

It's a simple question right? You'd think that the response would be pretty straightforward and clear. From my experience it is not. Why? Because most people are used to telling you what they DON'T want! We do it all day long, we complain about the weather, our weight, our job, and money we don't have. We complain about our boyfriends, our husbands, our boss, and all the people in our lives that treat us poorly.

The next time you're having coffee with that Negative Nelly friend of yours and she is complaining about what she doesn't want in her life, ask her this simple question:

What do you want?

I bet you she won't have a clear answer for you. Why? Because people spend way too much time focusing on what they don't want rather than what they do want.

The problem with complaining is that whatever we give our attention to, we get more of the same in return. This principle is based on the law of attraction. We attract what we feel, say and do.

So, the first step to getting what you want is in fact knowing what you want! As Zig Ziglar says "You cannot hit a target you can't see." We have to know where we are going in order to get there. This means we have to be perfectly clear about what we want or we'll never have it.

> *"IF YOU DON'T KNOW WHERE YOU'RE GOING, ANY ROAD WILL TAKE YOU THERE." - LEWIS CARROLL*

This is where getting clear is so important to goal setting. It's not enough to just keep it in your head. You need to write it down. We know that people with written goals have a much greater chance of achieving them than those who do not write them down. So what stops us? Lack of clarity; it's no surprise that if only 3 percent of adults have clear, written goals, that they are the ones accomplishing at least 5 times more in life than those who were not clear.

Clarity is the first and most important factor in determining success. High achievers and results oriented people know exactly where they are and where they are headed. They've formulated a plan to get there. The greater clarity you have the easier your path to success will be.

> *If you don't know where you're going, how will you know you've arrived?*

Thomas Carlyle once wrote "A person with a clear purpose will make progress on even the roughest road, a person with no purpose will make no progress on even the smoothest road."

This goal setting exercise comes from Brian Tracy's book "Eat That Frog". I've used this technique at many of my live workshops and seminars and it works exceptionally well.

Here's the plan on how to get clear:

1. Take a clear sheet of paper and make a list of the 10 things you want to accomplish this year.

2. State your goals in the present tense using I _____. Example: I earn x amount of money every month. I weigh _____ number of pounds.

3. Look closely at your list of goals and select the ONE goal that if you achieved it would have the BIGGEST impact on your life.

4. Whatever that goal is, write it on a separate sheet of paper, set a deadline and make a plan on how to achieve it. Brainstorm all the ways that you currently have in your arsenal based on what you know, with what you have, where you ARE RIGHT NOW.

Don't worry about having all the answers. When we set BIG GOALS we will not have all the steps clearly outlined. They will be revealed to us as we continue to take action and move in the direction of the goal. For now, do what you can with what you know. You can always do something. Take the first step. This exercise alone will transform your life.

CHAPTER 5

I CAN AND I WILL. WATCH ME.

My greatest pleasure in life is derived from doing what people say I cannot do.

Think back to when you were a little kid and you wanted to do something but your mom wouldn't let you. Didn't you want to prove her wrong, and make her see that you could do anything in the world and that you had no limitations? Of course you did. You couldn't understand why she thought you couldn't do something. Of course you could.

You see when you are a child you are a creature with no limits and no boundaries. If you think you are Superman, then you are Superman. If you think you are a princess that lives in a castle then you are just that.

What happens to us, as we get older is we keep hearing these words: No you can't, I don't think that's possible, are you crazy? You want to do what? I don't think you can do that? Etc., etc., blah blah blah! These words sink into our subconscious and we live life believing we can't or we shouldn't or even if we tried we never will succeed. Stop!

Be the girl who decided to go for it!

Get rid of other people's voices in your head. Even yours (the limiting beliefs only please)! I know this sounds odd, but you have to replace it with the belief that you can. You can, you can, YOU CAN. Whatever you want, you can have it.Whatever you want to do, you can do it. Sounds simple right? It is. Just believe.

If I told you that I had a magical genie that would grant you any wish your heart could come up with, would you go ahead and wish? Do it. But minus the genie, and replace it with the universe that is here to serve you and give you whatever it is you wish for.

To understand these concepts pick up a copy of "The Secret" by Rhonda Byrne. This book transformed my life. It will transform yours too.

You are what you believe yourself to be.

CHAPTER 6

BE YOUR OWN HERO

I had always been attracted to money, power, success and fame. But what I didn't believe is that I could be those things myself, and I always looked for them in someone else to make me happy. I was wrong. After having lunch with a wildly successful and extremely well known leader, I saw all these traits in him, but I was blind to see them in myself. The things we are seeking are seeking us, and this is when my sister said to me "why don't you be your own leader?"

Me? Be like him? But how could I? He's so successful, he's so smart, he has a whole team backing him, he's written a book, he's a huge philanthropist, and he's a billionaire with many successful businesses.

I'm just a girl, I don't have the resources, I certainly don't have the money, or the team, or, and I went on and on and on. My excuses spewed out of me like a never-ending faucet. Then I stopped to think for a moment. My sister was right, why couldn't I be like him? What were the reasons I was telling myself that I believed were true?

> *Be the change you want to see in the world.*
> GANDHI

That was an "ah ha" moment. Stop chasing what you think you can't be, and go and be that person yourself. Wow. When you get this one, the world is literally yours.

It all stems from a deep-rooted belief that I can't, I'm not good enough, and they're so much smarter than me. Wrong. Stop. You can do and be anything you set your mind to.

I repeat you can be and do anything you set your mind to. So I ask you this: What would you do if you knew you could not fail? If I could guarantee that you would not fail at whatever it was you wanted to do... I mean WHATEVER, what would you do or be? Think about it.

This is very powerful.

CHAPTER 7

WHO ARE YOU?

Let's start with the most important question you will ever ask yourself in your life.

Who am I?

This is one of THE most important questions you can ASK yourself and ANSWER.

How are you showing up in the world? What are people saying about you? What do you believe in? How do you carry yourself? What words form your sentences? How do others feel in your presence? How do you enter a room? How do you interact with others? What does your body language convey? What thoughts occupy your mind on a minute-to-minute basis? What are your best qualities?

All of these are vital questions to ask of yourself.

If you don't know the answers yet, here's a great exercise. There are a couple of ways you can go about gathering your research and learn more about who you are, what makes you YOU, and learn how you are showing up for other people.

Here's the plan:

One way to learn more about yourself is to do an anonymous survey and send it out to at least 25 people asking them to list your top 3 best qualities. You can use a free program called SurveyMonkey. Ask the simple question: Please take a few moments to list what you consider to be my best qualities? Then, wait for the responses to flood in. You'll notice that you will see the same descriptive adjective pop up time and time again!

You could also send an email to 10 people that know you well and ask this question: Your opinion is very important to me, I'd like to ask you how you would describe me and how you see me limiting myself?

Asking these questions will give you incredible insight into what is working well for you and what areas you need to improve on.

When I first started the Ladies WHO Lunch® Network, we put out a lot of fancy pictures on social media with women in beautiful clothes and what seemed to be a very luxurious lifestyle. The group instantly intimidated many people. I often heard, "Oh Maria I could never fit in to your group, everyone is so glamorous", and "I don't even know if I have the right dress to wear to one of your events". But when they actually attended the event and met me and all the other women, they told me that it was NOTHING like they anticipated. We were all friendly, and inspiring and supportive! I quickly took note and made some changes by adding other more casual events to show another side of the network, and to show who we really were.

> *The woman I was yesterday introduced me to the woman I am today, which makes me very excited to meet the woman I will become tomorrow.*

The ability to take and accept criticism is one of the best things you can do to improve who you are. This will move you to be the best version of you possible, which in turn will help you live your dream.

Take a moment to make a list of all the qualities that you would use to describe your best self version. Who are you? Do you describe yourself as powerful creative, intuitive, influential, kind, magnetic, sophisticated, glamorous, intelligent, passionate, confident, or grateful?

Choose 5 qualities of who you are as your BEST SELF, and write those down.

For me it would be:
    1. Inspiring
    2. Influential
    3. Powerful
    4. Motivational
    5. Ambitious

What about you? Who is the IDEAL YOU? How would you describe her using 5 adjectives?

Your job is to live out these qualities with intention on a day-to-day basis. How would you act if you were inspiring, powerful and influential? How would people treat you? You see, you are whoever you declare yourself to be! People will treat you accordingly in response to who you say you are.

I remember writing this book in a coffee shop and the server asked me what I was working on. I said I'm writing my book, and she responded with glee, "Oh! Are you an author?" My immediate reaction was to respond well no, I'm just trying to be, along with any other disempowering thoughts that were ready to pour out. I stopped myself. I responded, "Well yes! In fact I am an author, and I'm writing a best selling book teaching people how to live their dream." She beamed "How inspiring, I can't wait to read it and I'm sure it's going to be a huge hit!"

In order to bring our dream into existence we must act and feel as though it is ALREADY A REALITY.

She remembered who she was and the game changed.
LALAH DELIAH

Get to know yourself and stand firm in your beliefs and what make you YOU. This is the privilege of a lifetime.

"THE PRIVILEGE OF A LIFETIME IS TO BECOME WHO YOU TRULY ARE."– CARL GUSTAV JUNG

I know what I bring to the table so trust me when I say I am not afraid to eat alone.

#GirlWithAPlanBook

CHAPTER 8

WHAT DO YOU STAND FOR?

Do you know what you stand for?

The Girl With a Plan knows her values and what she believes. She rarely strays from them, and when she does a red flag goes up, indicating she is going in the wrong direction.

It's imperative that you find out what you stand for. What's important to you? What makes you unique? What do you believe in? Which values do you live by? Do you associate with those who share your similar belief system?

If you don't know what your values are and what's important to you, it's as though you're building a house on quicksand. You will never get very far or be successful.

People are happiest and most fulfilled when they are living in alignment with their values. Successful people are clear about what they believe and what they stand for and rarely deviate from these values. Unhappy people on the other hand are unclear and hazy about what they believe in making them confused and causing them to compromise their values constantly.

Why are values important?

We identify with those who believe what we believe. We want to be around people who think like us, and who uphold similar beliefs. This gives us a sense of harmony and ease and makes life flow.

Stress and unhappiness arise when we are not living our truth, when we compromise our values in some way. This can result from a relationship where two people do not share the same values. Happiness in a relationship is the result of two people sharing and living the same values.

You demonstrate your values in your behaviours and actions. It's not who you say you are, but rather the actions that you take that demonstrate to the world what you truly believe.

Like the expression goes, if you stand for nothing, you fall for everything.

A woman who knows her values is like a big tree with roots. She is so unshakeable that even the most powerful of storms will not be able to uproot her.

A person's values determine and shape his or her character and personality. They serve as the basis from which all actions stem and priorities are revealed. They dictate the kinds of relationships she will find herself in, and the kind of careers that will best suit her.

Values are often developed early in life based on your upbringing and the influences you had in your life. Values and beliefs can also be adopted later in life through many experiences. We have the ability to re-evaluate and modify as we grow into the person we were meant to become. What we choose to believe is entirely up to us.

A Girl With A Plan knows and lives her values on a daily basis.

When you are clear about your values you will find it much easier to say YES to all that is in alignment with them and NO to all that doesn't fit in the picture. To make your life easier, make sure you know what you stand for. What are your values? What do you believe in? What do you stand for and what will you not stand for?

The answers to these questions will largely determine your success in life and business.

Review the list of values in the Appendix of this book. See which ones jump out at you and which ones speak to you....

Choose 5 values that you believe in and write them down. Start the sentence like this:

I believe in _____

I believe in _____
I believe in _____
I believe in _____
I believe in _____

Having values that you believe in is the first step to building the foundation of a successful life and business.

When you know your values everything else becomes easy. Your values always serve as your base point and your compass. They are the place from which all decisions are made.

The values of the Ladies WHO Lunch® Network are:

FREEDOM, INDEPENDENCE, AUTHENTIC SELF-EXPRESSION, PASSION AND CONTRIBUTION.

These are also my personal values. You see, as the creator of the network my personal values are tied in with the company I have created. Yours should be too. What do you believe? Write your personal manifesto. Tape it somewhere you can look at it daily. Here is the Ladies WHO Lunch® Network manifesto:

We believe every woman has the power to create life on her own terms, in her own way, whatever that may look like for her.

We believe every woman has the right to live the life of her dreams.

We believe every woman has the right to be free. To not rely on anyone for her financial stability or her happiness.

We believe every woman has a choice and that she is not defined by her current circumstances, what others think of her and what society tells her she needs to be.

We believe that anything is possible, we are only held back by ourselves, and the limiting beliefs we keep telling ourselves.

We believe every woman is powerful, not only as an individual but collectively when we come together and see what's possible for ourselves.

We believe in taking 100% responsibility for our life and our success.

A woman who walks in purpose doesn't have to chase people or opportunities. Her light causes people and opportunities to pursue her.

Always look for the opportunity, not the obstacle.

#GirlWithAPlanBook

CHAPTER 9

WHAT DO YOU EXPECT?

You get out of life EXACTLY what you expect. If you expect success, you will have it. On the flip side, if you expect failure and unhappiness, you will have that too.

Have you ever heard of the Expectancy Theory (ET)? This is a theory that was first proposed by Victor Vroom from the Yale School of Management in 1964. Vroom's theory assumes that behavior results from the conscious choice.

Basically, ET (or expectancy theory of motivation) proposes an individual will behave or act in a certain way because they are motivated to select a specific behaviour over other behaviours due to what they expect the result of that selected behaviour will be.

The following study explains the power of what we expect to happen.

[1]Japanese scientists blindfolded a group of students. They told them that their right arms were being rubbed with a poison ivy plant. Yuck right?

Afterwards, all the students reacted with classic symptoms of Poison Ivy...itching, redness, boils (and, more). In reality it was only a harmless shrub that was in used.

On the other arm, actual poison ivy was used. This time they were told it was only a harmless shrub. An incredible thing happened. Only 2 of 13 students broke out with poison ivy symptoms! Amazing isn't it?

What we learn is that the expectations that the brain creates can be as real as those created by events in the real world. This is how the creation process works.

You get in life what you create. We are all creative beings and we constantly create in our daily lives. Our lives are a reflection of what we've created, that's easy enough to understand.

[1]In another example of the expectant theory, doctors in Texas conducted a study of arthroscopic knee surgery that used general anesthesia in which patients with sore, worn knees were assigned to one of three operations -- scraping out the knee joint, washing out the joint or doing nothing.

In the "nothing" operation, doctors anesthetized the patient, made three little cuts in the knee as if to insert the usual instruments and then PRETENDED TO OPERATE.

[1]Blakeslee, Sandra, "Placebos Prove So Powerful Even Experts Are Surprised; New Studies Explore the Brain's Triumph Over Reality", The New York Times, Oct 13, 1998, http://www.nytimes.com/1998/10/13/science/placebos-prove-so-powerful-even-experts-are-surprised-new-studies-explore-brain.html?scp=1&sq=poison+ivy+placebo&st=nyt&pagewanted=all

Two years after surgery, patients who underwent the sham surgery reported the same amount of relief from pain and swelling as those who had had the real operations.

A recent review of placebo-controlled studies of modern antidepressant drugs found that placebos and genuine drugs worked about as well. ''If you expect to get better, you will,'' said Dr. Irving Kirsch, a psychiatrist at the University of Connecticut who carried out the review.

So the question you have to ask yourself is:

What are YOU creating?

The answer is surprising: You create what you EXPECT. Expectation is what manifests into creation. What you expect is what you get.

Let's look at another famous study that highlights what I like to call "mental rehearsal" imagining things in your mind as you want them to play out. This famous study conducted study by Dr. Biasiotto at the University of Chicago takes a group of basketball players and splits them into 3 groups.

The 1st group practiced their free throws every day for 20 days.

The 2nd group didn't practice at all for 20 days.

The 3rd group only practiced successfully throwing free throws in their imagination for 20 minutes a day for 20 days.

They were all scored before and after the 20 days. The results were astounding!

The group that had no practice made no improvement. No surprise here right?

The group that practiced with a real ball improved 24%.

And the group that practiced only in their imagination improved 23%! The players who only practiced using their imaginations were activating their nervous system every time they visualized shooting a free throw. This mental practice conditioned their nervous system with what a successful free throw feels like, and so when it came to taking a real shot, their body responded the same way it did during the visualization.

I highly recommend a book called Psycho-Cybernetics by Dr. Maxwell Maltz it states: "When you see a thing clearly in your mind, your creative success mechanism within you takes over and does the job much better than you could do it by conscious effort or will power."

Maxwell Maltz was a plastic surgeon who discovered that it wasn't people's outer appearance that determined whether they were happy or successful but rather their own SELF IMAGE and what they thought about themselves.

We all have a self-image that dictates what we can and cannot accomplish and most of those thoughts live in our subconscious mind. All your actions, feelings, behaviours, and abilities are directly linked to your self-image.

Success in life boils down to how you feel about yourself. What image you hold of yourself and your capabilities in your mind at any given time.

What if we took a moment to tell ourselves of all the things that we're capable of and then actually believed them? What kind of results do you think you would be producing in your life if you expected to achieve all of the things that you desired. And yet, this is what successful people do: they BELIEVE and ACT as if it were impossible to fail and then they get to work taking the necessary actions that are in alignment with these beliefs and eventually without a doubt they reach their goal.

This rule is closely related to the Law of Attraction. We get what we feel. And if we feel and believe in our success then it can be no other way.

Here's your action step for today: What is ONE positive expectation that you have for today? Expect something that you really want today and see what happens!

WHAT YOU LOOK FOR DETERMINES WHAT YOU FIND

It really is all a matter of how you look at things. I love the expression, what you look for determines what you will find.

If you look for the bad, the bad will show up. Alternatively if you look for the good, the good shows up.

What we focus on in life and business is what we get. If we are continuously focused on how everything can go wrong and how nothing is going to work out, guess what we attract in our life? Yup, you got it, more of the same.

Train your brain to have a millionaire mindset. A mindset that always looks for the solution to the problem. A mindset that always answers the question: how can I make this work? A mindset that focuses on all that could go right.

I remember running out of adverting budget on a project.

Most people would give up and say ok well no more money left, let's quit. NO. It is simply an obstacle that we have to get through. I don't care if you go around, go through, jump over, knock it down. Whatever you do, obstacles are created for us so that we can get around them, not so they can stop us.

Every time you have a goal or dream that is big and scary for you, you will be confronted with roadblocks. Challenges. Things that don't go your way. What we have to realize is that this is completely normal.

The path to success is filled with potholes, bumps, and twists and turns along the way. It's what we do when we encounter these obstacles that will determine our success.

So, remember always ask HOW can I make this work? HOW can I get around this? HOW can I solve this problem? Brainstorm and get creative! You'll be surprised at what shows up when we look for it.

ENTREPRENEUR:

A crazy person who risks their own money for freedom, rather than exchanging their freedom for money.

#GirlWithAPlanBook

CHAPTER 10

BE UNREASONABLE

In order to change your life, change your circumstances and live your dream, you need to get MAD about it! Get angry about your current situation. If there's no fire or passion behind you attempting to change you're not going to do the things required to move you from where you are to where you want to be.

"AND THE DAY CAME WHEN THE RISK TO REMAIN TIGHT IN A BUD WAS MORE PAINFUL THAN THE RISK IT TOOK TO BLOSSOM." - ANAIS NIN

It's only when the PAIN of staying the same is greater than the pain of changing that we do something about it. It triggers us to take different actions than the ones we've been taking over and over again. Shaking us from being stuck in the same place.

It's only until you get to that point of absolute frustration, disgust and anger with your life and what's not working that you're actually going to take the necessary steps to change it.

I say get angry! If you're not angry about where you're at, you're not going to change! You'll remain comfortably uncomfortable. Say NO to the status quo of your current situation.

YOU'RE BEING UNREASONABLE

Be unreasonable! When's the last time you heard someone say this to you?

I'm sure a lot of you never heard this while growing up either, and may even continue to hear this instead: oh come on, be reasonable - you can't do that!

In fact, I can bet you still hear it today. Mostly from family, from people who play it safe, from people who feel it's better to stay where they are, and who think people who take risks are crazy.

I hate it when people tell me to be reasonable. It rubs me the wrong way! Why should I be reasonable about my goals and dreams?

The majority of the population uses a safety net. Playing safe so that they don't get hurt or disappointed when and if they don't achieve their goals. You know what I say? It's better to have tried and risk looking a fool then to have never tried at all and remain looking safe.

> *"IT IS IMPOSSIBLE TO LIVE WITHOUT FAILING AT SOMETHING, UNLESS YOU LIVE SO CAUTIOUSLY THAT YOU MIGHT AS WELL NOT HAVE LIVED AT ALL, IN WHICH CASE YOU HAVE FAILED BY DEFAULT."* JK ROWLING

I want to dance in the rain. I want to work on my passion project day and night. I BELIEVE with every fibre of my being that it will be successful. I want to spend every dollar I earn and invest it back into my business. I know that's what it takes to be successful.

I am the girl who started a business with no money, no resources and nothing but a beat up computer from her kitchen table in her small apartment while trying to raise her young son as a single mommy.

I am the girl who nobody thought could do it and in the end she ruled her world.

I continue to want to be all of those things, and I want the same for you. I want you to be unreasonable in your desires and your dreams and your aspirations.

If you are keeping company with people who are going to tell you to be reasonable and stick to what is safe, you're in the wrong room. Get and stay away from these people. Far far away. Instead, surround yourself with people who will encourage you to dream big, to do things that scare you, and make you step out of your comfort zone.

Here's the thing, if you keep doing what you're doing, you will keep getting the same results that you've been getting. So, I ask you, how's that going for you? I'm going to assume that you want to create bigger, different, better results for your life and that's why you picked up this book.

You didn't pick up this book because you want to be reasonable - you are a Girl With A Plan who wants to get somewhere by being unreasonable.

I remember taking a self-development class back in 2012 and the first thing the teacher would say to us when we walked in was not how are you today? But rather: What are you being unreasonable about today?

Reasonable people do not change the world.

Unreasonable is waking up at 5am every morning to work on your passion project before the kids are up for school and while everyone else is asleep.

Unreasonable is disconnecting your TV set and committing to reading a book a week!

Unreasonable is following your heart and staying true to who you are when everyone else thinks you're crazy.

Unreasonable is working 2 jobs to finance your dream.

Unreasonable is leading when everyone else is following.

Unreasonable is taking a risk and not being afraid to fail.

Unreasonable is doing what most people won't in order to have what most people don't.

"What if I fail?"
Oh my darling, but what if you fly?

Don't get to the end and wish you had.

#GirlWithAPlanBook

CHAPTER 11

WHAT'S IT GOING TO TAKE

What's it going to take for you to change your life and be the person that you dream of?

Is it going to take you losing a girlfriend or boyfriend? Or losing a husband, or wife? A best friend? How about losing years of your life that you will never get back?

What's it going to take to make you realize that you have a limited amount of time on this earth and that your runway of life will end at some point.

What has to fall on your head to make you realize that something needs to change?

God is always nudging us in more ways than we know. If only we'd look and listen more carefully.

In the beginning it's just a whisper, a feeling that you need to change something in your life. We often ignore this whisper and hope it goes away. Things are just fine. We lie to ourselves. Then, we feel a slight tap on the shoulder, and think hey who was that? Go away, I'm doing just fine I don't need you to tell me what to do.

For some of us, unfortunately the whisper turns into a catastrophic wake up call. As though a big brick falls directly on our head. Some will survive. Others don't. This kind of impact cannot be ignored. This is it, if you've survived this kind of blow then you're one of the lucky ones and you have a chance to start over. Do better, do differently.

Our chances in life are limited. We are limited by the number of days we have on this earth. Why do you think you have forever to make the changes necessary today? Why do you keep putting off what you need to do today to get you to where you want to be tomorrow? The answer is because you think you have time.

The answer is because you think you have forever. That there will always be a second chance. That there will always be another opportunity. But what if there wasn't? What if this is it? What if this were your last chance? Would you take it or sit on the sidelines and watch it go by? Will you get to the end of your life and wish you had?

Don't wait until a brick falls on your head. Don't wait to get to the end only to wish you had taken a chance on your dreams.

Here's the plan. Envision what you want your perfect life to look like. Imagine that you have a magic genie personally assigned to you and your every wish was her command.

Answer the following questions:

1. What do you want your life to look like?
2. How do you want to wake up feeling?
3. How do you want to feel in your life day to day?
4. How do you want people to describe you?
5. How would you spend your time?

CHAPTER 12

THE ONLY DIFFERENCE

The only difference between you and me, is that I think I can and you think you can't. That's it. Once you get this, you can create and have anything you have ever dreamed possible. That's it. This belief has to be so ingrained and unconscious for you that there is no disputing it. You can. You just can.

When you know this to be the utmost truth without a spec of disbelief you have just become the most powerful person in your life. Notice how I said your life? There is a key distinction here. You see for many years I walked around with the belief that others who were more successful were that way because they were smarter than me, had better education than me, went to special schools, had good mentors. I made up whatever story I could come up with.

Who cares if they did or they didn't. I assumed that they had something that I didn't and the fact is, I believed they COULD and I COULDN'T. That was the difference.

When I finally came to the powerful realization, that I was responsible for my own power and success, I finally got it. No one is better than you. You just think they are for whatever reason or story you have made up. Once you let that go and understand that they just might have as much insecurity as you do, it will all make sense. They don't have it all figured out, you just think they do.

So, if you think you can, you are right. Definitely right!

ACT AS IF

One of the greatest strategies for success is to act as if you already have what you want.

This means that you act and behave in a way that signals to the universe that your desire is already in your possession.

How do you do this? Well, think about what you would do if you were already living the life you envision? How would you walk? How would you talk to people? What would you be thinking? How would you be acting? How would you feel about yourself?

Acting as if sends powerful commands to your subconscious mind to elicit creative ways to match who you're being. It helps activate what is called the Reticular Activating System (RAS) where your brain starts noticing anything around you that will help you succeed. Start acting like whoever it is you want to become, and soon you will become that person.

Ever since I can remember I've dreamed about having a mentor. I dreamed of having someone I could look up to, learn from and turn to for guidance. I never believed I could make this happen until I started using this technique. I started pretending like I had the best mentor possible, someone so powerful and influential and so successful that I would be on top of the world if he or she would mentor me, and then I started acting like this was already the case. Now at this time, I didn't have an exact person in mind, but I was very clear about who he or she had to be. It had to be someone who had achieved the level of success that I aspired to. Someone I admired and respected and if that person mentored me I would literally be screaming with joy from the rooftops.

I began compiling a list of questions that I would ask my mentor, I began to imagine him or her writing a review for this book. I even imagined sitting in a particular restaurant having lunch with my mentor and what that would feel like! After just a few short weeks of walking around like I had a mentor, I was at a conference on leadership in Vancouver, BC with some impactful female speakers. This included Jessica Herrin and Kirstine Stewart both of whom I had the pleasure of meeting afterwards. Sitting two seats away from me was a young lady who I started a conversation with. At the time I had no idea who she was. I thought maybe she was a young aspiring female entrepreneur here to take in the insights of the day and so I asked her how she was enjoying the conference so far.

Turns out that she had been following me on social media and she knew who I was. I love it when that happens (never underestimate the power of social media). I was honoured and then I asked her what she did. She replied I'm the executive assistant to Peter Legge. Now that name rang a bell and I knew that he was somehow associated with one of my favourite magazines, BC Business!

We exchanged a few more words then had to focus on the next speaker. A few weeks later, the young lady sent me a message on Instagram inviting me to be her guest at the upcoming Top 100 BC Business Event hosted by BC Business at the Fairmont Hotel. Peter would be interviewing the legendary David Foster, a philanthropist and multi grammy winner. What an honour! Of course I said yes and I was there with bells on.

Later that week she also sent me an email inviting me to be on the Executive Committee of the 30th Annual David Foster Miracle Gala in support of the David Foster Foundation that Peter Legge would be the Chair of. Wow, I nearly fell off my seat, this was certainly the opportunity of a lifetime and I immediately said YES!

With this acceptance I had the privilege to meet Peter and sit next to him in a few intimate Executive Committee meetings. During this time and prior I soaked up as many of his books as I could (he has authored 21 so far!) and each time I would meet him I would get him to autograph one of his books. I knew that he read a book a week diligently and considered him to be one of the most successful business men in Canada. This must surely be a secret to his success, so I increased my once a month book read to reading a book a week as well.

At the end of about our 3rd meeting, I contemplated something very bold, and it started with this question that EVERYONE should be asking themselves on a daily basis:

What if?

What if I asked Peter to be my mentor?

What would happen? The mere thought of it made my palms sweaty and my heart beat faster. Then all the fears and doubts swooshed over me like a tidal wave. Why would Peter want to mentor me? What right do I have to ask a man of his caliber and power such a question? What if he laughs at me? What if he is insulted? The questions came fast and furious and ran through my head like a stampede.

But then came the ultimate question: What if he said YES?

I felt butterflies in my stomach and my head spun with possibility and elation! Yes, what if he actually said yes? Now that would be a miracle!

I remembered 3 statements of truth that I had shared with my network the previous day and I decided to take my own advice.

Here they are:

1. If you don't go after what you want, you'll never have it.

2. If you do not ask, the answer will always be NO.

3. If you do not step forward, you'll always be in the same place.

> *Life has no remote, you need to get up and change it yourself.*

I don't remember my exact words, but it went something like this: Peter as a leader I'm always mentoring others and I have never had a true live in person mentor except virtually and through books. I'm sure you get asked this constantly and your time is extremely valuable and limited but would you consider being my mentor?

And then I paused and never felt more alive, excited and scared all rolled into one.

He answered: YES.

I almost fell off my chair, and so it was, he would start mentoring starting in the fall over lunch. I was to bring him a set of specific questions and he would answer them for me, but he said I must be diligent and put into practice what he taught me otherwise there was no point to our meeting.

I agreed and left the meeting feeling like I was walking on air.

Acting as if had paid off in the most magnificent of ways. You see, as soon as I started to act as if I had a mentor, the universe responded by providing me one - the powerful Law of Attraction in action.

The Law of Attraction simply states that what you think about you bring about. The more you create the vibration, which is just the mental and emotional state of already having what you desire, the faster you will attract it to you.

If you believe you can do a thing or you believe you can't, either way you're probably right.

#GirlWithAPlanBook

CHAPTER 13

BRAINWASH YOURSELF

In order to reach the level of success that you want, you will need to brainwash yourself. You're probably thinking, brainwash myself? How the heck do I do that, and WHY would I want to do that?

Either way you will be brainwashed whether you like it or not, but the question is, who is the one doing the brainwashing? If you want to achieve your dream and reach your goals then it has to be YOU. You have to brainwash yourself.

Brainwashing is by definition the act of penetrating and infiltrating your subconscious mind on a continual basis until it accepts what you are feeding it as truth.

Florence Shovel Shinn, author of The Game of Life and How to Play It said: "If you do not run your subconscious mind yourself, someone else will run it for you."

The media, particularly social media these days wants to brainwash you. Advertising companies want to brainwash you, as do certain religions. Around 20 billion a year is spent on advertising to try to get into your subconscious mind. They understand that once they get into your subconscious, where your belief system and your paradigms are held that they have a small level of control over your decision making.

Once you have control over someone's mind, you control what they choose to create in their reality. Knowing this, wouldn't you want to be the one brainwashing yourself? The obvious answer is YES!

Let's look at how we can successfully brainwash ourselves and learn to control our subconscious minds for the purpose of living our dream and creating whatever reality we want.

"CONTROL YOUR MIND OR IT WILL CONTROL YOU."

In order to re-program our mind with a new belief that will serve us, we need to activate repetition. Studies show that it takes a minimum of 21 days to form a new habit or belief.

Let's get started. Here's the plan:

We must first understand how the subconscious mind works. Your subconscious mind is extremely powerful but also very vulnerable in that it believes everything you feed it.

There was a study done by Dr. Lee Pulos that revealed in one second of time, the conscious mind uses about 2 thousand neurons. In that SAME second, the subconscious mind uses 4 billion neurons. This means that in every second of our lives, there are 2,000 neurons making "conscious" decisions and 4 billion neurons making "subconscious" decisions. Can you see who's in control?

To further illustrate the power of the subconscious mind over the conscious mind I highly recommend "The Ant and The Elephant" by Vince Poscente.

Here are some facts about the subconscious mind:

1. The subconscious mind is always ON even when you don't think so. It is always picking up and recording EVERYTHING it sees and hears.

2. The subconscious mind has been referred to as the theater of the mind because it records and stores all information and mental movies of your life.

3. The subconscious mind does not understand the words, don't, no and not. For example if you say: I will not eat sugary treats, the image that appears in your mind is that of sugary treats, thus you will continue to think sugary treats.

4. The subconscious does not operate in the future. It only exists in the NOW, the present tense. That is why it is so important that when we speak about our goals, we need to visualize them as already accomplished. When you talk about your desires start your sentence with: I have, I am, I make, I weigh.

5. Our subconscious mind controls 95% of our lives, it controls our habits and as we know, humans are creatures of habit. 95% of what you thought and said yesterday, you also thought and said today. So that leaves the conscious mind with only 5% of airtime. Not very much is it? Do you see now which mind we need to influence more?

6. The subconscious mind cannot tell the difference between your imagination and reality.

7. The way to form new beliefs in the subconscious mind is by REPETITION. If you repeat anything long enough to yourself, you will eventually start to believe it.

So here is the key, if all this is true, then it is evident that you ATTRACT all the things that you place into your subconscious mind. This is called the Law of Attraction. It states that we draw to us whatever we give our attention, energy and focus too. So we can draw to us what we feel. Your thoughts and feelings are a form of energy that will attract to you exactly what you think.

"WE DON'T ATTRACT WHAT WE WANT, WE ATTRACT WHAT WE FEEL."

Since our subconscious mind is made up of habits, we tend to think the same thoughts over and over and this is why we end up with the same reality over and over again. In order to change your reality, you will need to re-program your subconscious mind. This is why you need to brainwash yourself.

Here are the steps to make this happen:

1. Clearly write down exactly what you desire. Write it out in detail but make sure you state it in the present tense.

2. Imagine yourself already having what it is that your desire. Make mental movies in your mind and imagine what it would feel like to already have what it is you desire. Try to include as much detail as possible, including colors, sounds, touch, taste and feel. Play these movies out as if they were already real. Remember the subconscious mind cannot tell the difference between a visualization and what is real.

3. Take a break from social media and watching the news. Only give your attention and energy to the things that align with your desired outcome. I have a set of cue cards that I read every morning and every night religiously. They contain affirmations that are important to me. Here are some examples of my daily affirmations:

I am allowing what no longer serves my highest good to peacefully dissolve and effortlessly melt away.

I keep my attention on what I want to create.

My heart is light. I have forgiven everyone who has hurt me and I am free.

I am committed to be a person who is happy every single day no matter what happens.

I am capable of accomplishing anything I place my attention upon.

Everyday my income increases whether I am working, playing or sleeping.

I am super laser focused on what I want to achieve and I maximize every minute of my time.

If I can conceive of it, passion and the abilities to create it will be given.

And my mantra:

1. Think well of all.

2. Be cheerful with all.

3. Dwell day by day in thoughts of peace toward every living creature.

4. Create an empowering affirmations for yourself that when spoken imply that you are already in possession of what you want. Repeat this over and over in the morning and at night before you go to bed and thought the day. Affirmations should be stated in the present tense just like goals, starting with I have or I am. Remembering that the subconscious only operates in the present tense.

5. This step is one of my favourites. Create a positive affirmation stated in the present tense of whatever your dream or desired state is and set it as a reminder on your phone! Let is come up daily every hour on the hour. When you see the reminder, speak the affirmation out loud. Do this for at least 21 days. This new belief will sink into your subconscious and you will take actions in alignment with this new thought pattern bringing you closer to your dream.

After surviving a very difficult break up while writing this book, I had programmed the following affirmation *"I'm getting better and better every day in every way"* to display on my phone every hour! At first I didn't believe it as the pain was so strong I thought it would never go away, but I kept repeating it over and over until I finally believed it and the affirmation became the truth.

6. Talk as if you have already achieved your goal and dream. Act as if, remember your reality follows your imagination.

7. Rinse and repeat. New habits and beliefs are formed through repetition. Consistent implementation is the key to success with affirmations.

If you follow these steps outlined above, you will successfully brainwash yourself to put you in the right mindset to achieve all your goals and dreams.

To obtain your goal, you must take the reins of your subconscious and lead and guide them in ways that benefit you.

When you declare daily that you're receiving, your words make a believer out of your subconscious mind, which then starts working with you to help make it so!

CHAPTER 14

THE VOICE IN YOUR HEAD

We become what we think about.

The first time I heard this expression I wasn't exactly sure what it meant.

Here's the best definition I can give. We are driven by our thoughts. Everything we do or do not do is because of a thought that we have. This thought which is held in our mind, is like a tape that plays over and over prompting us to take or not take the action that ultimately leads to our results.

That voice in your head that you may or may not be aware of is referred to as the subconscious mind. A mind so powerful that it can move mountains. A mind also so powerful that it can also keep you stuck in the same place forever without knowing why.

So how do we change and control our thoughts to achieve the results that we want? It has been said that the average person has about 60,000 thoughts a day. We obviously cannot control every single one, however we can control the dominant ones. The dominant thoughts that keep showing up over and over to impede our progress and success.

How? Simple. Simple but not easy.

First, by being AWARE. When we are aware of our thoughts we then immediately have the power to change them. Awareness is the key to all transformation.

Ultimately here is my simple formula for transforming thoughts: Change the words that you are using.

WORDS = THOUGHTS = FEELINGS = VIBRATIONS = RESULTS

When you change your words, your thoughts change and that puts you in a different vibrational energy. Now, as we know, it has been proven, you attract what you feel, and when this happens your results change.

Our words carry so much power and weight that we do not realize it. Words have the power to destroy. But, they also have the power to create! Choose your words wisely and consciously on a daily basis.

You will become whatever you tell yourself you are. Think about that one for a minute. You become whatever you believe yourself to be, and people will respond to you as who you SAY YOU ARE.

Here's the secret if you want to transform your life it comes down to this one strategy:

Train your mind to think differently.

Have you heard the expression that the definition of insanity is doing the same thing over and over again and expecting different results? It's the same thing with our thoughts. We cannot think the same things and expect to achieve different results. If we want to transform our lives we need to think and choose different thoughts. This thinking in a certain way will create different actions, which will create different behaviours, which in turn will produce different results.

Control your thoughts or they will control you.

And let's face it, isn't this the reason you're reading this book? You want to produce a different result for yourself? Your results don't lie. You either are where you want to be or you're not, it's that simple.

There's always a reason why you are where you are. Why you've attracted the people, places and things into your life that are there right now. Every relationship every situation is a mirror for who you are.

According to the law of attraction, you attract what you FEEL so once you raise your vibration to the level of what you want to receive, all that is not in alignment with who you are being will naturally leave your life.

You are always just one thought away from changing the rest of your life. All you have to do is hold that thought continuously until it becomes your reality.

Reality is indifferent to our perceptions of it. Reality has no meaning, it is not biased, it just is. Each person's perception of reality however is different. Situations and events have no meaning other than the meaning YOU assign to them. This is a good thing because we can CHOOSE how we respond to what is. For example two different people can interpret one event in two entirely different ways even though the event was the same.

Often times what we think is the worst thing that is happening to us is a blessing in disguise. Try to change your perspective on events that happen to you and see them from a different angle.

"WHEN YOU CHANGE THE WAY YOU LOOK AT THINGS, THE THINGS YOU LOOK AT CHANGE." – JIM ROHN

One of my favourite books for reprogramming your mind for success: The Power of I AM, Joel Osteen.

WHAT SUCCESSFUL PEOPLE EAT FOR BREAKFAST

The way you start your day defines your day. Your mind needs brain food. In the morning feed your mind, not just your body.

Every successful person I know has a morning routine that they stick to religiously. Why? This practice sets them up for their day. It lays a foundation for the events of the day, and I have often heard it being called the most treasured time away from everyone else. A time to reflect, think, plan, meditate, set goals, nourish our minds and express gratitude.

I'm an early riser. I'm usually up at 5:00am but easily in bed by 8pm. Kinda crazy right? I often joke and say I don't work 9 to 5 like most people, I work 5 to 9. What I mean by that is, I'm working on my dream from the moment I wake up until I fall into a deep restful sleep and wake up the next day and do it all again.

I remember working for Bob Rennie, known as the condo king here in Vancouver. He had taken the team out for lunch one day to congratulate us on making and exceeding our real estate quota for a particular project. When I asked him what his secret to success was, he said he woke up at 4:30am every morning! At first I thought I misheard him. 4:30am? Who wakes up at 4:30am? Multimillionaires that's who. If you look at Bob's success it's easy to see that he falls in this category. He's also early to bed and never takes meetings in the evening.

So, it's true that early birds do catch the worm. You'll be hard pressed to find a CEO that sleeps in past 7am.

For me, the morning is my most productive time. A time of reflection, a time of routine, structure, self-improvement, meditation, big picture thinking, goal setting, scripting, and planning my day based on my priorities.

If you want to develop morning routines that will set you up for success, I recommend The Miracle Morning by Hal Elrod and The Perfect Day Formula by Craig Ballantyne, both excellent reads.

This is what my morning routine looks like: (roughly around 30 minutes)

Start by meditating for 5 minutes (I have plans to increase this, sitting still continues to be a challenge for me)

Visualize for 5 minutes on what I want to create and see it as already happening

Give gratitude for 3 things/people in my life

Read my affirmations on cue cards

Read my book for the week 10 minutes

Watch a short inspirational video

Write and review my monthly goals on one page

Look at my TO DO list (which I've made from night before) and prioritize tasks

Set my intention for the day.

We've all heard the expression: you are what you eat. It's the same way with your mind, whatever thoughts you feed your mind, you will become.

Stay away from negative people. They have a problem for every solution.

#GirlWithAPlanBook

CHAPTER 15

SAY GOODBYE TO NEGATIVE NELLY

You've heard it said many times. Misery loves company. It's easier to complain than to actually do something to change your circumstances. Right? Wrong. Not YOU. Not a girl with a plan.

When it comes to my work with the Law of Attraction, and in my course She's in Biz Blueprint, I always begin by asking people what they want. I mean WHAT DO YOU REALLY REALLY WANT? You'd be surprised at how many people don't actually know the answer to this question. In my online courses we get clear on what that is.

To learn more about my programs and how they can help you visit www.IdeaToRealityCourse.com which focuses on using the Law of Attraction to get crystal clear about what you want and then attracting it to you! If you're an aspiring female entrepreneur with an idea that you want to make a reality, then www.ShesInBizBlueprint.com is the place for you.

The universe can't give you what you don't know you want. Imagine pulling up to a drive through window. You begin your order something like this "I'd like to have a small coffee, no make that a large, actually I changed my mind, I'd like a milkshake instead!" Wait, no, milkshakes are fattening, let's go back to the coffee, on second thought, do you have orange juice?"

You get the idea. The cashier on the other side would get pretty fed up with you right? Even worse, based on all your changes, you might even get the wrong order! Yet, unfortunately this is how people approach life and their goals and dreams. But, not you, not a Girl With A Plan. A Girl With A Plan is crystal clear about what she wants and can identify it very clearly. She is not wishy washy and she is not indecisive. She is straightforward with her desires and knows her target.

"YOU CAN'T HIT A TARGET YOU CAN'T SEE." – BRIAN TRACY

Let's get back to the Negative Nellys. Why do people complain? Ever thought of that? Because it's easier to complain than to actually DO something about changing your situation. Complaining is easy. It means you accept no responsibility for the way things are. It means there is always someone else or something else at fault with the way things are. Complaining has no power and gets you nowhere, except in the company of other complainers.

I noticed something. When people get together in groups, mostly at work, particularly at a job they don't like, they complain. They complain to each other, and the more they complain the more they have to complain about. I remember hating to listen to them. It was like cacophony to my ears. I just wanted to open my mouth and say well then DO SOMETHING ABOUT IT!

What people don't realize is that they actually DO have the power to change the things they complain about otherwise they wouldn't complain about them! We don't complain about what we can't change. We only complain about the things that we do have the power to change.

And you know why people don't change? I've discovered it's because of 1 of these 3 reasons or a combination of all:

1. They don't know how to change, they don't have the tools, they haven't read the books, and they don't know how to get into the right mindset. This one is pretty easy to fix. Every skill is learnable if you apply yourself. Every mindset is learnable if you openly adopt it.

2. They know what they have to do but are too lazy to actually take the necessary action. You can fix being lazy too, it's called taking action. It's called pushing yourself to do the things that you don't feel like doing, but that will yield you the greatest results.

3. They don't have enough discipline to implement the necessary steps to change their lives. Jim Rohn once said: There are 2 kinds of pain in this world. The pain of discipline and the pain of regret. The pain of discipline weighs ounces, the pain of regret weighs TONS.

Everyone wants to be successful until they really understand and see what it takes to be successful. Successful people did not get to where they are by being lazy or resting on their laurels. They are some of the biggest action takers that exist.

Ask yourself this question: What are you willing to do that most people won't in order to get what most people will never have?

I can't stress enough how important it is to watch the company you keep. You've heard the expression "don't let the naysayers drag you down" and stop hanging out with the Negative Nellys! You need to put yourself in an environment that consists of people who lift you up instead of drag you down. You want to consciously surround yourself with people who see the extraordinary in you, who see the limitlessness of your abilities and potential.

This is one of the main reasons I created the Ladies WHO Lunch® Network, to purposefully surround myself with women who are supportive, positive and like-minded. When you immerse yourself in this kind of environment, you're on the right path to greatness. To learn more about this global community of encouraging and inspiring women visit www.LWLNetwork.com to receive an exclusive invitation and find out how this international network can help YOU reach your goals.

How do you know you're hanging out with negative people? It's easy, you know by how you feel. When you are in their company and after you've left you are feeling heavy, discouraged and deflated and you are left feeling less inspired. After such encounters you tend to focus more on the problems rather than the solutions.

A person with a negative mindset will influence you and will leave you feeling disillusioned and drained. That's not where you want to be.

My advice is to try to distance yourself as much as possible from these people. It's not that they're bad people. This is their mindset and they might not know any better. They definitely have not been trained to think differently.

The success of you, your business and goals ALWAYS depends on who you surround yourself with. So be very careful who you let into your life on a daily basis. Don't let the Negative Nellies drag you down.

Each of us is what we are because of the dominating thoughts we permit to occupy in our minds.

#GirlWithAPlanBook

CHAPTER 16

THE EVICTION NOTICE

Anything that is not congruent with your truth and what you believe needs to be EVICTED from your life.

Let go of the people and situations that are not aligned with your values and what you believe in. As painful as this might be, in order to get closer to who you truly are it's a must.

To know yourself is the greatest gift you can ever give yourself. When you know yourself you will be unshaken, you will stand tall and proud, even if it means standing alone. There will be winds and storms but you'll never be broken, you'll never fall once you are firmly planted and rooted in the truth of knowing who you are and what you stand for.

You can't get to where you need to go if you're still taking that same road. You know the one. The one you think is going to lead somewhere but all it does is circle you back to the same place you started.

Get off that road. Choose another path. The new path will look scary because you haven't been down it before. Anything that is not familiar to us is uncomfortable. The path will call you until you can't ignore it anymore or until you become so dizzy from constantly going round in circles that you will have no choice but to choose this other path.

How will you know you're on the wrong path? You know by how you feel. It's the little voice that you want to ignore but can't because it's always there.

How will you know which path to choose? As long as you are taking actions that are in harmony with your values and what you believe, the path will be shown to you. You will know you're on the right one when it feels easy and when you are actually getting somewhere. When you are no longer stuck in the same place, new opportunities will come to you and you will marvel at all the things you see along the way.

But remember you will never set foot on this journey if you continue to lie to yourself and stay on the path that is familiar to you.

Don't be afraid of the pain of letting certain people and situations go. Without the pain you will never discover your ultimate destiny.

Give notice as politely and as peacefully as you can and then let your actions do the speaking. Stop sounding like a broken record and actually do it.

Your words carry no weight if they are not followed by the actions. Action is the only remedy for getting off the dead end street.

Your greatest transformation comes from ending something. It comes from making it final. You'll only change when the pain of staying the same is bigger than the fear of transforming. Let the universe know you are done with this, and ready for THAT!

CHAPTER 17

DON'T BE A ZOMBIE

Ever notice how every successful individual has a clearly defined purpose? A reason for being, a reason for getting out of bed in the morning a reason for every action in their day.

Successful people live with intention, clarity, purpose and direction.

You cannot be successful if you do not clearly define your goals and then take purposeful actions on a day-to-day basis to achieve them.

Life is something that YOU CREATE by the actions you CHOOSE to take and the thoughts you CHOOSE to think. Live life on purpose, not by accident. Take one look around and you see many of us walk around like zombies. People are in a complete state of disengagement, resignation, and hopelessness. This makes me so sad but it also makes me angry! Get angry! Don't be a zombie! Stop thinking that life is something that happens TO YOU; Start creating.

> "SUCCESSFUL PEOPLE DON'T LET THINGS HAPPEN TO THEM, THEY GO OUT AND HAPPEN TO THINGS."

There's only one person that can change your life and that person is YOU. You and only you have the power to create your life that way you want it to be and no one else. NO one else is responsible for your happiness. Once you realize this, you are truly free. Free to create on a blank slate, because you hold the paintbrush. You hold the pen to the book of your life. You can write what goes into each chapter, what fills the pages of your life. Let me ask you right now, if your life were a book, would you want to read it?

> "I TRUST THE NEXT CHAPTER OF MY LIFE BECAUSE I KNOW THE AUTHOR."

So you're probably thinking ok how do I create the change I want? You do it ON PURPOSE. With intent and focus.

I'm a huge fan of writing down your goals and each day I write the top 10 most important things that I need to accomplish to get me closer to my dreams. And I keep this list with me everywhere I go. If I'm on the computer, it's right next to me, if I go out I put the notebook in my bag. It is a constant reminder to me to STAY ON TRACK.

Live your life with purpose, on purpose.

It is this tenacity, and relentless determination that allows me to achieve as much as I do. So here's how I stay on track and live life on purpose.

If and when I feel myself drifting (trust me, I can drift and be swept away by shiny object syndrome quite easily), I stop myself and look at my list and I ask myself this very important question that has changed my life and will change yours too:

IS WHAT I'M DOING RIGHT NOW IN THIS MOMENT CONTRIBUTING TO THE REALIZATION OF MY GOALS?

Then I look at my notebook. If the answer is no, I know I need to STOP and get back on track.

This is the only way to reach your goals and live your dream. ON PURPOSE. You do not live a life by accident, success is not an accident, it's very deliberate and calculated. I used to think that successful people had some magic formula that I didn't know about and if I could just get my hands on it everything would fall into place.

There is no overnight success, people are not born successful, they are made. Made through consistent, deliberate, purposeful actions taken on a daily basis.

CHAPTER 18

TUNNEL VISION

All success comes from clarity.

Being really clear about what it is you want and then taking the necessary steps to make it happen. If you don't know where you're going, how will you know when you get there?

So many people wish they had more money, a bigger house, a better car, the ability to go on vacations every year and not worry about bills. These are not goals they are merely wishes. A wish doesn't have anything to stand on. A goal is an action plan with clear, concise steps and a deadline.

Knowing what you want, and being able to identify the roadmap to achieving it clearly is the fundamental ingredient to your success.

When you get clear on what it is you want, you start developing tunnel vision. What this allows you to do is to really stay focused on what's important to you, because you KNOW what's important to you. Do you see the difference? How can you stay focused on something if you don't know what that something is?

Starve your distractions, feed your focus.

When you become focused on what it is that you want, you will not become distracted by the things that are not important and not a part of your clear vision.

When you focus on doing something you love, everything else that doesn't matter –doesn't matter.

So again the key is to get really clear on what you want as this will allow your mind to discard all that is not important and not in alignment with your desired outcome. Your mind will discard what's not important, and the reason it discards it is because you've told it what you DO want!

Until you get really clear on what you want, you will fall for everything and be swayed and pulled in a million different directions, which will ultimately lead to a life of unhappiness and frustration.

Tunnel vision is when you're really clear about what you want, and everything that you don't, doesn't enter into the tunnel. It doesn't enter into the tunnel because it's not meant to be there. It's not meant to be there because you are now clear about what you're allowing into your life and what you are not. This is where the power lies.

Once you develop tunnel vision it'll be easy to let go of the people, places, things, situations that don't serve you and your highest greatest good, and that are not in alignment with who you are and where it is you want to go.

Sit down and take time to clearly identify what makes you happy. When I ask this question to people a lot of times they have no idea. Some might think they know but it's not until they start peeling away all of the layers of the onion that they discover what it is they truly want.

So start by asking questions to discover who you are.

> What makes me happy?
> What will I tolerate and not tolerate in my life?
> Where do I find my greatest joy?
> When is it that I am mostly my authentic self?
> Where do my strengths shine through?
> What do other people say about me and how do they compliment me?
> What kinds of questions do people ask me?
> What kinds of things do people say I'm good at?

You want to ask these questions when it comes to your career.

> *"IT'S A BEAUTIFUL THING WHEN A CAREER AND A PASSION COME TOGETHER".*

On the personal side of things particularly in relationships, it's important to know exactly what it is you want in a mate. I recommend "The Soulmate Secret by Arielle Ford" to really help you get clear in this area if you're not already.

You have to start by asking yourself why you're attracted to a certain person. Often times friends will be dating a guy who they are attracted to but who is not particularity a nice person and I will ask them, what is it about this guy that you find attractive?

Often their answer is that they are attracted because they feel the chemistry and the passion. To this I say ok great, so you want to feel passion and sparks, but what about the other stuff? Do you want him to be unreliable, non-committal, and dishonest?

And, they say "No, of course not!" So I ask them why they believe that they can't have it all? The passion, the trust, and the commitment all rolled into one?

The answer is that they don't think it's possible. But, I'm here to tell you that it is. Don't settle for anything less than what it is you want and believe. Believe without a shadow of a doubt that you can and will have it. No excuses, no ands, ifs or buts.

The Girl With A Plan has enough self-confidence to walk away from relationships that don't serve her. She believes without a shadow of a doubt that by walking away from what isn't working she clears the path to receive what will work to enter her life. She knows, she can't move forward when she keeps looking back. She lets go, believes and trusts that what she seeks is seeking her. She knows it won't be able to find her if she's still stuck in the past. She gets in alignment with what she wants, so it can appear.

I love Wayne Dyer's book "Excuses Begone!: How to Change Lifelong, Self-Defeating Thinking Habits" where he refers to excuses as mind viruses that have infected, infiltrated and have multiplied taking residence in our subconscious mind. These mind viruses have been learned at a young age through our environments and conditioning. They are not true.

You have the ability to design your life, your relationships, your career any way that you want it to look. It all boils down to setting a clear intention, and then taking the steps to make that happen. When you actively participate in this daily intention, the people, circumstances and situations that are not meant to be in your life will easily fall away. They are not going to come into the tunnel with you, there simply won't be enough room for them.

Here's an affirmation that I use daily that can help you too:

"I AM ALLOWING WHAT NO LONGER SERVES MY HIGHEST GOOD TO PEACEFULLY DISSOLVE AND EFFORTLESSLY MELT AWAY. I AM FREE."

Put this affirmation on a cue card and carry it around with you everywhere you go, reading it multiple times a day.

What would you do if you knew you could not fail?

#GirlWithAPlanBook

CHAPTER 19

IMPOSSIBLE TO FAIL

What would you do if you knew you could not fail?

I remember the first time I came across this question. It was in a book by Canadian author Barb Stegemann. What a weird question I thought. I've never been asked that before! I thought about it. What would I do if I knew I couldn't fail?

She asked, how would you act, how would you be? How would you walk and talk differently?

Have you heard the expression "fake it till you make it?" When you act as if, you're activating the law of attraction, which simply states: you attract what you FEEL. Think about that: YOU ATTRACT WHAT YOU FEEL.

So if you are feeling successful, you will attract more success into your life. If you are feeling wealthy and abundant you will attract more abundance into your life. If you are feeling love, you will attract love.

When you act a certain way, you feel a certain way. When you see yourself as a success, you attract more opportunities that are in alignment with that vibration. You carry yourself a certain way, you project a certain energy. It's that energy that draws more of what you want towards you.

One of the greatest strategies for success is to act as if you are already have what you want.

This means that you act and behave in a way that signals to the universe that your desire is already in your possession.

How do you do this? Well, think about what you would do if you were already living the life you envision? How would you walk? How would you talk to people? What would you be thinking? How would you be acting? How would you feel about yourself? What would you be saying?

This is where acting as if comes in. By acting as if you send powerful commands to your subconscious mind. When you do, you'll elicit creative ways to match who you are being. This behaviour helps activate what is known as your Reticular Activating System (RAS). Your brain will notice anything around you that will help you succeed. Start acting like whoever it is you want to become, and soon you will become that person.

The Law of Attraction simply states that what you think about you bring about. The more you create the vibration, which is just the mental and emotional state of already having what you desire, the faster you will attract it to you.

> *EVERYTHING IS ENERGY AND THAT'S ALL THERE IS TO IT. MATCH THE FREQUENCY OF THE REALITY YOU WANT AND YOU CANNOT HELP BUT GET THAT REALITY. IT CAN BE NO OTHER WAY. THIS IS NOT PHILOSOPHY. THIS IS PHYSICS." - ALBERT EINSTEIN*

Remember that whatever we give our attention energy and focus to expands. When we sit around all day long and think of all the things that won't work, we are feeding our fears, doubts and insecurities. Guess what happens? They EXPAND.

They take over, they pull us into a vortex and they bring us more of the same.

Instead, banish those un-serving, untrue thoughts and replace them with the feeling of everything going right.

Visualize your day, your life unfolding exactly as you imagine it. Really get into that feeling. Also pay close attention to whom you are spending your time with.

I like the way my friend and powerhouse Meredith Powell puts it: "Invest in the people who pour water on the fires of your fears and throw gas on the passions of your dreams."

When other people see our potential and what we are capable of, it ignites our own self-belief and we move forward in faith. Have you ever doubted yourself and your ability to do something and then heard a friend say, you can easily do that, you are so powerful! Having people who believe in us propels us forward and moves us closer to achieving all that we were created to do.

> *"SURROUND YOURSELF WITH THOSE THAT SEE THAT GREATNESS IN YOU EVEN WHEN YOU DON'T SEE IT FOR YOURSELF."*

When you have others who believe in you, it gives you the energy to take action despite your fears. This was one of the fundamental reasons I started the Ladies WHO Lunch®Network, to be around a group of women who focused only on the positive and who encouraged others to do the same. Whatever we give our attention, energy and focus to will expand, regardless if it's positive or negative. Why not start focusing on all the things that can go right rather than all the things that can go wrong.

What are you focusing on today and how is it affecting your life?

CHAPTER 20

ATTITUDE VS IQ

I remember when I started my entrepreneurial journey. I used to look at others who had the success that I was looking for and I used to think: What does she have that I don't? I was clearly convinced that others had some secret formula or were equipped with a brain that I did not have that allowed them to achieve that level of success! I really believed I was lacking in something.

But the honest truth is that I absolutely WASN'T, and neither are YOU!

> *"THAT SOME ACHIEVE GREAT SUCCESS IS PROOF TO ALL THAT OTHERS CAN ACHIEVE IT AS WELL." - ABRAHAM LINCOLN*
>
> *"I'M JUST A GIRL WHO DECIDED TO GO FOR IT."*

It is normal to look up to the people we admire and want to be like and to assume that we can't get the same results. Perhaps we think that these people have been gifted with a special type of brain or that they have some kind of superior intelligence that we could never access. Nothing could be further from the truth. There IS something however that distinguishes those that succeed and others that fail and that is ATTITUDE.

Attitude is always more important than IQ so pick a good one!

> *"YOUR ATTITUDE, NOT YOUR APTITUDE WILL DETERMINE YOUR ALTITUDE." – ZIG ZIGLAR*

There was a study conducted at Stanford University that proved that it was not IQ that contributed to success but rather ATTITUDE. When it came down to it, people fell into one of 2 mindset categories, and these 2 mindsets determine the level of your success in life.

A bad attitude is like a flat tire. You can't go anywhere until you change it.

The first mindset is the fixed mindset. The average person has this mindset. The fixed mindset is characterized by pointing fingers and laying the blame on someone else. Those with this mindset are set in their ways and don't believe they have any control over or the power to change their attitude, behaviour or life. These are people stuck in fear. They don't believe in change or growth of any kind.

The second mindset is the growth mindset that successful people embody. The people in this mindset believe and understand that they are NOT their circumstances and will NOT be defined by them. They know that they have the power and ability to make the necessary changes in their lives in order to lead them down the path to success. The growth mindset doesn't look at failure as a reason to give up but rather as feedback and necessary lessons to move forward and grow.

The most important factor in determining one's success is how one handles failure. Successful people know that failures and setbacks in life and business are unavoidable. They know it's how one reacts to these situations that will reflect whether one is successful or not.

"YOUR ATTITUDE DETERMINES YOUR ALTITUDE. HOW HIGH YOU WANT TO GO IS ALMOST ENTIRELY DUE TO A POSITIVE ATTITUDE."

Let's take a look at the 5 habits that "growth mindset" people display on a daily basis. You can use all of these habits to embed more success into your life:

1. Do more than the average person does. Average efforts will get you average results. Work while they sleep. Learn while they party. Hustle while they play. Then live like they dream.

2. Never complain. You can EASILY tell who is stuck in the fixed mindset by how often they complain. You will rarely hear successful people complain if at all. Why? Because they are focusing on how to solve problems. They're not thinking about what they can't do about a given situation. One of the

questions I continually ask myself is not, WHY can't I make this work, but HOW can I make this work. Successful people are solution oriented rather than problem focused.

3. Take chances and be ok with uncertainty. The life of an entrepreneur is by no means a straight and narrow one. If you're looking for straight and narrow then you should probably stick to your 9 to 5. Entrepreneurs take risks, a lot of risks without any guarantee that it is going to pay off.

4. Focus on what you want to happen, not what you don't want to happen. Growth mindset people say goodbye to the negative chatter that tells them they can't do something and instead focus on the outcome that they want to become reality. The law of attraction clearly states that whatever we give our attention to whether positive or negative we get. So really start thinking about where and what you're putting your focus on.

5. Take consistent action! When setting out to achieve your dreams, know that inconsistent action is not going to get you the results you want! Growth mindset people take massive consistent action day after day even when they don't feel like it, even when they are tired, and yes even when they feel like giving up. Success doesn't happen overnight, it's all about being patient, and the journey of a thousand miles really does start with a single step.

When I first started the Ladies WHO Lunch® Network we started with ONE member. Today 5 years later we have a global community that continues to grow daily.

DON'T GET TO THE END AND WISH YOU HAD

I use this expression often, and although morbid, it illustrates a key theme of this book. What would your life look like if you weren't afraid to live it?

"I'D RATHER LIVE A LIFE OF "OH WELL" RATHER THAN "WHAT IF."

"I'D RATHER REGRET THE THINGS I'VE DONE THAN REGRET THE THINGS I HAVEN'T DONE."

Bronnie Ware Authored "The Top Five Regrets of the Dying", her memoir of a career spent working in palliative care. She shares with us the #1 regret of those at the end of their runway of life. Here it is:

I WISH I'D HAD THE COURAGE TO LIVE A LIFE TRUE TO MYSELF, NOT THE LIFE OTHERS EXPECTED OF ME.

"This was the most common regret of all. When people realize that their life is almost over and look back clearly on it, it is easy to see how many dreams have gone unfulfilled. Most people had not honoured even a half of their dreams and had to die knowing that it was due to choices they had made, or not made. Health brings a freedom very few realize, until they no longer have it."

What's your greatest regret so far, and what will you set out to achieve or change before you die?

CHAPTER 21

GETTING TO KNOW

FOR YOU TO BE INTERESTING, YOU HAVE TO BE INTERESTED.

I highly recommend that you get to know yourself.

Why? No one wants to be around someone who has nothing to say. What are you interested in? I mean really ask yourself these questions, and then know the answers to them! Share your own opinion, not just what you THINK someone wants to hear.

If we just met and I said to you: tell me 7 random things about you. You have 30 seconds. Go. Would this be something you would struggle with? Why? How well do you really know yourself?

Please get to know yourself, and then share that with whoever wants to listen. True happiness comes from knowing yourself so well that even you would love yourself if you were someone else.

Are you a republican or a democrat? Do you believe in abortion or pro-life? Do you like chocolate or vanilla? Are you a night owl or an early bird? Do you believe in love at first sight?

You must have the answers to all these questions. If you don't know yourself, how can you expect anyone else to get to know you.

Until you truly know yourself, happiness will elude you.

My life is based on a true story.

HEAR BUT DON'T LISTEN

Listen to others but don't listen if it conflicts with what your heart is telling you.

Truly successful people follow that voice inside them. That gut feeling that leads their heart to make the right decision.

Don't be easily swayed or discouraged by the opinions of others. Everyone has one. Yours is really the only one that matters. Don't let anyone else think for you. You can do that on your own. Women are luckier than men in this area.

We naturally have something we called women's intuition. It RARELY lies. Well, if I have to be truly honest, I ignore it only when I don't want to listen to it, and always I wish that I had. Be still, listen to it, it will not steer you wrong.

Holding on to anger is like grasping a hot coal with the intent of throwing it at someone else; you are the one who gets burned.

BUDDHA

#GirlWithAPlanBook

CHAPTER 22

BRING IT TO THE TOP AND LET IT GO

Whatever eats at you will eventually kill you. Whatever is bothering you, you must bring it to the surface. What I mean is don't stuff it down, don't suppress it, and for God sakes definitely don't pretend like it's not there.

Whatever it is that you're holding onto, bring it to the surface and don't let it fester. The more you keep things inside, the more they build until you are so blocked up that you can't see anything in front of you.

Say you have resentment towards someone. This one is huge because most of us have it without even realizing it. Identify it, and let it go. Identifying it might be the easy part. How do I let it go you ask?

Confront, talk about it, tell the person how you feel, shine light on it, and then, let it go. Just drop it. You see it's never what they said or did that holds you back, but it's your interpretation of what they said or did. Have no interpretation of whatever it is. They did what they did or they said what they said to you. That's it. Don't attach any meaning to it.

My ex husband used to say, "Mur, resentment is the pill I swallow hoping you'll die." Resentment doesn't hurt anyone but the person feeling it.

"Picking up a hot coal with the intention of throwing it at someone else only hurts you." - Gandhi

Once you realize that these emotions are holding you back, you will quickly let go of them.

Would you rather be angry or would you rather be rich?

You choose. I did.

CHAPTER 23

COMPETITION IS FOR COPYCATS

If you want to lead a happy life then you need to stop comparing yourself to others.

Comparison is the ultimate thief of happiness. The moment we compare ourselves to someone else is the moment we lose our power.

You might be surprised - the people that you compare yourself to might be comparing themselves to YOU! Remember everyone is portraying an image to the world of how they want to be viewed. This is far from the perfect picture of them that you have in your mind.

Comparing yourself to others is a no win situation. It's a downward spiral that has no meaning but to deter you from where you want to go. Look ahead, not next to you or behind you.

There was a beautiful girl that I used to compare myself to. She had everything I didn't, or so it appeared. It was getting ridiculous at one point. I would focus so intently on what she had going on that I completely lost track of the direction of my life and the gifts that I had to offer this world. The minute I decided to stop worrying about what she was up to and focus on how I could make my life better, she seemed less important, actually pretty insignificant. This was the moment I got my power back. It's weird, how that happens.

I keep my focus on making my life better and off other peoples behavior.

Do you ever wonder why racehorses have blinders on? It's so that they can focus on keeping their eye on the finish line. If they turn to their right and to their left constantly worrying about what the other horses are doing, they would lose concentration and ultimately lose the race.

Don't worry about what others around you are doing. The less you place your attention on them, the less influence they will exert over your life, emotions and energy. A true winner looks forward and inward never to the left and right. Keep your eye on the prize, it's yours.

When you concentrate on making yourself a better person, everything that is trivial falls to the wayside, and the only thing you can see is your goal of the most fabulous you possible. So the next time you're tempted to see what everyone else is doing, stop and put that energy back on yourself and what YOU need to do in this present moment to make your dream a reality. Give it a try. It works.

> *Because she competes with no one, no one can compete with her.*

Stop comparing your behind the scenes to everyone else's show reel. Things aren't as they seem on the outside, particularly with the rise of social media where everyone is portraying only the side of them that they want you to see which is not necessarily the every day, down in the trenches, real life struggles that we all go through.

When you are truly coming from a place of authenticity and creativity there really is no competition. No one can compete with someone who creates purely from the heart with their eyes shut and nothing but their own vision.

It's easy to spot the copycats. They're everywhere. These are people who lack self-confidence, who believe that they don't have what it takes and who are always looking left and right seeing what everyone else is doing and trying to figure out a way to incorporate that into their business.

I remember when I started the Ladies WHO Lunch® Network in December of 2012. I had a vision for creating a movement, a forum where women could get together both online and off to support, encourage and inspire each other to live out their dreams.

Our first live event was FANCY! I mean boy was it ever fancy! I had everyone wear big hats and fascinators. We had a huge buffet lunch, a fashion show and speakers. I think there were more photographers there than guests! It was a big deal. I kind of describe it like a wedding although I was marrying myself.

At the end of the event, people said "Wow! This was amazing!" and "When is the next one?" To be honest at the time I didn't have any plans to host another event, this was really just a one off thing to prove to myself that I could take something from idea to inception and be successful at it.

OH no Maria! You really have something here, the ladies had so much fun, you MUST continue with this!

To this day LWL is still going strong and is committed to the success of female entrepreneurs all over the world. The question I get asked all the time is simply this: What gave you the idea to start LWL? Did you go to different networking groups and pick and choose what you liked about them and what you didn't and then came up with the concept for LWL? Ha-ha, no not at all. In fact, I had never even been to a networking event in my life!

You see LWL wasn't born out of what other people were doing. It was a passion and a desire deep inside me to connect and inspire women to get past all their limiting beliefs. Here I could show them how truly beautiful and powerful they were not only as individuals, but when came together collectively to discover new possibilities for ourselves.

Since then many groups have tried to emulate our success and our model. I like to say, imitation is the highest form of flattery. However, it is also the downfall of your business. The moment you try to compete with someone is the moment you've lost your power. You weren't born to fit in, God made you to stand out. If you were born to be like everyone else then we would have all looked exactly the same!

One of the values of the LWL Network is authentic self-expression, be who you are and don't worry about what others will think of you. Confidence is powerful. Girls with a plan are always powerful.

Creative people don't worry about copycats because they can create faster than copycats can copy. March to the beat of your own drum and you'll always be the leader.

I don't believe in competing for what I want; I believe in creating what I want.

In order for you to be successful you don't need to take anything away from someone else.

Life is not about what happens to you but how you choose to respond to what happens to you.

#GirlWithAPlanBook

CHAPTER 24

THE POWER IS IN THE RESPONSE

Mastering your emotions and controlling the way you react to what happens to you in life is one of the most challenging things we can do to grow as human beings and cultivate our character.

As emotional beings we are reactive. That's just the way it is. Some of us are more than others. And yes, I am referring to my Greek heritage and how I can be extremely fiery and passionately reactive.

While passion is a good thing and can be put to great use for many positive outcomes, too much emotion not channeled in the right way can be destructive.

Let's face it, as much as we would like to we can NEVER control what is happening around us or to us at any given moment. Trust me I've tried, many times and have come up short always. I have caused myself a lot of grief, and frustration trying to figure out why things didn't work out the way I planned them.

Hello! Wake up call, life doesn't work like that. We cannot control people or mold situations and outcomes into what we want them to look like. This was really hard for me to get as I am a self-proclaimed former control freak. I let that go.

The simple lesson here is that you'll never be able to control everything. Nor should you want to. That's where the beauty in life lies. In the unknown to some extent, in having faith that God is steering you in the right direction and accepting where you are right now.

I'm not talking about not making goals and taking the steps to make sure they happen. What I'm saying is at some point we need to let go of the outcome.

When you can't control what's happening around you, challenge yourself to control the way you respond to what's happening. This is where your power is.

A woman that is unshaken and has deep roots and stands tall like a beautiful tree will not be swayed by windstorms.

The power is in your choice. We always have a choice as to HOW we respond to what is happening to us. Is this easy, hell no! Does it take practice, yes it most certainly does.

Your power lies in your choice and the way you choose to respond at any given moment. Trust me, that lesson will keep showing up until you get it right.

Another handy technique is to use reframing. Try to reframe what you think is a negative situation into a positive one. Remember events are just events, words are just words, it's how we interpret these things that gives them meaning. Keep in mind that reality is indifferent to our perceptions of it. Each individual makes meaning based on their beliefs and mindset.

So choose a response that empowers you. A response that makes you feel strong and powerful. Choose to respond with dignity, class and elegance. Smile through the pain and wish your worst enemies all the best. When you bless your enemies you rob them of their ammunition to hurt you. They become powerless. This is when you become truly untouchable and undefeated.

This is my personal mantra:

"THINK WELL OF ALL. BE CHEERFUL WITH ALL. DWELL DAY-BY-DAY IN THOUGHTS OF PEACE TOWARD EVERY LIVING CREATURE."

CHAPTER 25

SQUARE PEGS DON'T FIT IN ROUND HOLES

I cannot tell you how many times I tried to do this in my younger years. Fitting square pegs into round holes. I spent countless amounts of energy and time trying to understand why something was not working out and what I could do to make it work.

I didn't understand that square pegs do NOT fit in round holes. I kept thinking there must be a way I can make this work, I'm smart, I'm creative, he'll change, the situation will change, something will shift, and finally it'll work out the way I intend it too.

Well, that was absolutely futile and a big waste of precious energy. Some would also call it stubborn. Others maybe even naive. I see it now as a combination of the two, not to mention an extreme case of being a control freak.

There's an expression that I'd like to share that illustrates this point: "The definition of insanity is doing the same thing over and over again expecting different results"

It just doesn't happen, all you do is drive yourself crazy.

So how does this apply to life and business?

In life this was evident in my early relationships where I would think that somehow I had the magic formula or recipe for trying to change someone into the person I wanted them to be rather than looking for what I wanted in someone else.

A part of that is the teacher in me, always trying to help, always trying to fix things, make things better, to help people to see their true potential.

But here's the reality: you can lead a horse to water, but you can't make it drink.

And boy! Would I ever get upset when they wouldn't drink the water. What's wrong with you I would think? I've shown you the way, I've highlighted all that needs changing and fixing, now why aren't you drinking?

Unfortunately the problem wasn't with them. It ultimately resided with my actions and me. Instead of trying to change others, focus on making YOU better.

Through the years, I've learned to shift my attention from what is not working to what is then I've asked for more of that in my life!

I stopped telling the universe what I didn't want in a relationship and started voicing what I DID want. Not just voicing but writing it down. Actually sitting down and making a list. A very carefully thought out list of all the qualities and the ways I wanted to feel in a relationship.

Once I started doing this, an amazing thing happened. The universe made space for that to show up in my life. Both personally, and in business.

The moment you get really clear on what it is you DO want, trying to fit the square peg in the round hole will never be an issue again. You will never feel frustrated at things not working out, you will just sigh, look back at your list and say NEXT! You will be actively making space for what truly belongs in your life rather than forcing something that was never meant to be there in the first place.

I believe the universe moves you through different relationships and situations in order for you to learn. This is so that you become the person you're meant to be. Yes, there are lessons that will need to be repeated several times before we get it. So if you're wondering why you're always dating the same kind of guy or why certain things ALWAYS happen to you and how unfair life is, my guess is it's because you haven't learned the lesson yet. This situation will keep showing up until you finally do.

In business, when I first started the Ladies WHO Lunch® Network all I knew was that I wanted to inspire women to live a fearless and fabulous life and to go after their dreams. Unfortunately I had NO idea how I was going to do this, and I didn't know what that was going to look like. When we have big dreams we won't know how it's all going to unfold, but we must get ourselves into action and take the step forward. Stop talking about it and start doing. Do something, anything, just do.

In business we must remain fluid to the outcome and not be set in what we think the outcome should look like. I've tried many things in my business to help the network grow and to provide value to the women. Some things have worked really well and others have flopped. The important thing is to keep your eye on the big picture, your WHY, the reason you are doing what you're doing, and you must hang on very loosely to the HOW that executes and plays out.

Don't get stuck on a business idea that you think is working when clearly it's not. Shift your attention, change direction, try something new.

I had the pleasure of meeting and hearing David Foster, a famous music producer and 16 time Grammy winner speak in Vancouver for the BC Business Top 100 event. Peter Legge, interviewed him and this is what David said about keeping up with the changing times:

"Retreat and attack in a different direction"

When something is not working out, stop driving yourself crazy by trying to fit the square peg in the round hole. Try something different. Do it differently, see it from a different angle, try something new.

I promise the results will be transformational and worth it.

CHAPTER 26

FALL DOWN SEVEN, GET UP EIGHT

In life we will encounter many setbacks and challenges. Some of us more than others. The difference is what we do after a setback, and how we react. What we can learn from it, and what we can takeaway from the whole experience.

Brian Tracy says setbacks and challenges are not there to obstruct but rather to instruct. The key is to keep moving forward after the setback.

"EVERY SETBACK IS A SET UP FOR A COMEBACK."

We will all stumble in life and we will all fail, and if we don't then we are not truly living, but merely alive.

"YOU MIGHT NEVER FAIL ON THE SCALE THAT I DID, BUT SOME FAILURE IN LIFE IS INEVITABLE. IT IS IMPOSSIBLE TO LIVE WITHOUT FAILING AT SOMETHING, UNLESS YOU LIVE SO CAUTIOUSLY THAT YOU MIGHT AS

WELL NOT HAVE LIVED AT ALL - IN WHICH CASE YOU FAIL BY DEFAULT." –JK ROWLING

Growth doesn't come from standing still. It comes from falling flat on your face, time and time again. I believe those that fail are the most successful people out there.

Why? Because each time they are knocked down they don't stay down for very long, they take the lesson, dust off and get right back up again. This builds resilience, perseverance, strength, and determination. All characteristics for success.

" *I MAY PAUSE BUT I WILL NEVER STOP.*"

Being defeated is often a temporary condition. Giving up is what makes it permanent.

CHAPTER 27

INTERESTED VS. COMMITTED

Are you committed to your success or just interested?

It makes all the difference. Everyone is interested in being rich but very few people are willing to put in the work to get there. Anyone can be interested, that's easy, however very few people can stay committed, and that's hard.

Most people if asked the question "Do you want to increase your income?" would answer YES of course, however these people are just interested in having more money, which means that they take action only when it's convenient.

It is the committed that do great things in life, the committed who reach their goals and dreams, it's the committed who change the world. A Girl With A Plan is committed to achieving her goal, not just interested. When you are committed to producing results there are NO EXCUSES, you find the time, you carve out the time, you do whatever needs to be done to get into action and to accomplish what you said you needed to do. The committed are creatures of habit. Good habits that lead to breakthroughs and success.

> "WHAT ARE YOU WILLING TO DO THAT MOST PEOPLE WON'T IN ORDER TO GET WHAT MOST PEOPLE NEVER HAVE."- LES BROWN

In January of 2014 my son and I made a decision to disconnect our TV and haven't gone back since. We thought it might be difficult at first but to be honest it was a lot easier than we thought.

> "POOR PEOPLE HAVE BIG TVS, RICH PEOPLE HAVE BIG LIBRARIES" – JIM ROHN.

I also read somewhere that people who don't watch TV accomplish much more than those that don't and ever since then I made the decision to be one of those people. The number one question I get asked often is "how do you do all that you do?" And my answer is usually quite simple: I don't have TV.

Being committed to making your dream happen means doing anything and everything you can to stay the course come hell or high water to do what needs to be done.

> "COMMITMENT IS STAYING LOYAL TO WHAT YOU SAID YOU WOULD DO LONG AFTER THE MOOD YOU SAID IT IN HAS LEFT YOU."

Your actions will always determine your results. Committed people do what it takes even when they don't feel like it, even when the motivation has left them. This is the definition of commitment. It's the ability to do the things we say we're going to do regardless of how we feel. People who are just interested don't have this kind of investment. They are not invested, they are interested. If success happens great, if it doesn't that's ok too. Committed individuals see success as their duty. Success is their obligation, and they will not sway when the winds blow.

Most people go through life being interested in goals. They are not committed to doing the work that is necessary to achieve them. Being committed means believing without a shadow of a doubt that you will achieve whatever you set your mind to, no matter what.

When you're interested in doing something you do it only when it's convenient, however when you're committed to something you accept no excuses. Only results.

Let's take the classic example of losing weight and getting more fit. Let's say I'm interested in doing this, which most people are. If I'm just interested I will only eat healthy and go to the gym when it's convenient for me. The idea of eating healthy and going to the gym sounds good, but I'm not committed to it, just interested in it. If you're interested in something rather than committed you'll find yourself making a ton of excuses. I didn't go to the gym because I was tired that day, or the kids were acting up or I couldn't find a baby sitter, or it just didn't fit into my busy day.

When you're committed you will throw out the excuses and tell yourself that nothing will get in your way. You won't make excuses. Excuses are for the interested. Results are for the committed.

A river cuts through a rock not because of its power but because of its persistence.

Committed people don't put things in front of their goals and dreams and it shows in their actions. Let's say you've made a commitment to work harder in your business and make more sales, but your boyfriend wants to take you out to a movie that wasn't planned. A committed individual will stay focused on the commitment she made to herself to work on her business, an interested individual will say sure why not, I can always get to my work another time.

Committed people are really clear on what needs to get done in their business to move them forward and they will not easily be swayed by other's agendas.

Excuses fall on deaf ears of the committed because they know that if they really want something, nothing is going to get in their way. Committed people find time to do the things that actually matter.

We always find time, money and resources to do what we truly want to do.

So think about your goals and dreams and ask yourself this question? Am I committed to making them happen or am I just interested? If the answer is committed then you will accept no excuse and you will do whatever it takes to accomplish them.

Committed people have no interest in being interested. So you might be asking how do I go from interested to committed?

Here's the plan:

1. KNOW YOUR WHY

To be committed you have to know your WHY, your raison d'être, the reason you do what you do. The thing that makes you want to jump out of bed in the morning. Your reason for living! If you don't know what your WHY is, I recommend you watch Simon Sinek's famous youtube video "Start with WHY". So what's your WHY? Peel away all the layers of the onion to really get to the core of why you do what you do. I also recommend the She's in Biz Blueprint where we devote an entire module to figuring this out! More at www.ShesInBizBlueprint.com

2. BE COMMITTED

When you know your WHY and what you stand for, this easily leads you into commitment!

3. TAKE CONSISTENT ACTION

Commitment easily leads to action, when you're committed you DO! You take consistent action on a daily basis to get you the results that you desire!

Ask yourself this question: Am I interested in achieving my dreams, or am I committed to achieving my dreams? Remember interested people only do something when they feel like it. Committed people on the other hand do something with passion and purpose and look to produce results every single day no matter what. Which one are you?

This will be by far the single most important question you can ask in your lifetime.

CHAPTER 28

YOU ARE THE PROBLEM AND THE SOLUTION

So often we look outside ourselves to try to understand why things aren't working. We blame our family, our boss, our partners, our living conditions, the cards we've been dealt, and the struggles we've had to endure. We complain about the way things are and act like it's someone else's problem.

The hardest thing we can do is take responsibility for our actions, because it is our actions that have or have not produced the results that are currently present in our lives.

The proof is in the pudding. We either have reached our goals or we have not. We either live in the house that we want or we do not. We either have the relationship we want or we don't. We are either living our dream or we are not.

When we point the finger at someone what we don't realize is that we have 3 pointing right back at us. What does that mean? It means that we are the creators of our life, of our situation of our problems. That's the bad news.

The good news is that we also are the solution! YES, that's right, no one else can do that for you. No one else can give you your dream life, your dream business. You have to do that for yourself.

Whatever problem you are experiencing now know that you are also the solution to that problem or difficulty.

It all starts and ends with YOU. You, that person you look at in the mirror every day. You are so powerful. You have the power to destroy but you also have the power to create. It's sad that our society and the human race as a whole choose defeat and failure over taking action and taking responsibility.

This was so hard for me to grasp. I remember having pretty much everything, big house, fancy cars, live in house keepers, vacations and pretty much anything anyone could ask for, until one day that was taken away from me very unexpectedly. I ended up in a tiny apartment that was a far cry from the 5,000 square foot mansion that I used to live in.

I remember blaming everyone I could think of, particularly my ex-husband for my current circumstances. I remember thinking how ALL OF this was HIS FAULT. I recall taking a personal development class and one of the teachers telling us that everything was a CHOICE. That we had the power to create or change our lives based on our choices. I remember thinking so vividly "Yeah right, I CERTAINLY did not choose to live in this tiny apartment".

Then he turned to me and said, circumstances may have brought you to live in that apartment, but it's your choice whether you remain there or not. You have no idea how angry that made me.

I didn't choose to live here I said, this is a choice that I was forced into! He said yes, temporarily but you still living there is YOUR CHOICE.

Don't spend half your life telling people what you're going to do and the other half explaining why you didn't do it.

Wow, I really struggled with this, and when I finally understood the lesson I had the power to change my choice.

Repeat after me: "My current situation is NOT my final destination."

The key to all transformation is AWARENESS. Once you are aware of the thought patterns that are holding you back, you ultimately have the power to change them.

We are constantly CHOOSING. That is where our power lies as individuals, as creators of our life and destiny and dreams.

Every choice we make whether consciously or subconsciously is shaping our future, that is why it is vital to ask yourself on a daily basis, usually hourly is best, sometimes even moment-by-moment.

Are the choices I'm making today getting me to where I want to be tomorrow?

The results don't lie.

YOU ARE YOUR CHOICES

What you choose is who you are.

Bad choices create bad habits. Bad habits one on top of the other are the obstacles and roadblocks to your success.

> "GOOD HABITS ARE HARD TO FORM BUT EASY TO LIVE WITH. BAD HABITS ARE EASILY FORMED AND HARD TO LIVE WITH." - BRIAN TRACY

A great life is made up of small seemingly insignificant choices on a daily even hourly basis that add up and contribute to a big life!

I was at the grocery store the other day just after my jog and noticed that my choices that day at the till were all healthy. I chuckled and said to the cashier "I'm not always this healthy, some days I just want to eat ice cream."

Then I realized that the choices we make directly impact our results in life. If you want to change your life make different choices.

Good choices are not easy to make. It's not easy to choose an apple over a slice of cake, or to get up an hour earlier to run instead of stay in your warm bed, or to stay at home and study while your friends are out having fun.

These choices are somewhat of a sacrifice, but nothing great comes easy.

Here's the good news, the more you make better choices, the easier it becomes. The better choices start forming into habits, and once that is done, there's no breaking those! Habits form the foundation of our lives. What we repeatedly do day in day out equals who we are.

To become more aware of the choices that you are making on a daily basis you could do a time log. For a week write down EVERYTHING that you do on an hourly basis. Then write your goals down. Make the connection. Do your actions point towards your goals? This is an eye opening exercise. Start today.

Be the energy you want to attract.

#GirlWithAPlanBook

CHAPTER 29

THIS IS THE LAW

I remember sitting in my hairdresser's chair back in 2008. This is when I first heard about the Law of Attraction.

He had told me of a story of two sisters who had read a book called "The Secret", listened to an audio about it every day and had manifested everything on their desire list!

Really I thought? How crazy this sounded. How could it be so easy? Of course my first thought was of pure skepticism. If they are doing it and it is working for them then how come everyone else isn't onto this?

If this is a tool that can be used to change your life why isn't everyone doing it? And so I became intrigued and got my first copy of the book that made the Law of Attraction such a huge success called "The Secret", by Rhonda Byrne.

I have to admit the first time I read it I wasn't really sure that it sunk in. In fact, I ended up reading it 4 times, until I finally began to realize how the law worked and how I could use it to my advantage.

Here is a simple definition of the Law of Attraction:

You can attract either negative or positive experiences or people into your life based on your thoughts and intentions. Whatever you think most about will eventually manifest into your life. So if you focus on problems you will attract more of the same. On the flip side, if you focus on solutions and the good things in your life you will find opportunities. Our thoughts have always created our reality.

If you are actively employing this universal truth, it will work. Here are a few ways to notice the evidence of it working.

1. YOU ARE LESS RESISTANT TO CHANGE.

You may have heard the expression, what you resist, persists. Don't fight the changes in your life, they are there for a reason, they are signaling you that you are no longer in alignment with those people, places, situations or things that are now moving away from you. Change is vital for growth. Life is always changing, we can either fight it or accept it. Don't hang on to the past, be open to letting it go to make room for the positive. When you resist change you only re-create more of the negative experience you are holding on to because you can't let go of the past. Change happens for a reason, usually to clear out negativity from our lives and replace it with positive people and experiences.

2. YOU ARE LESS STRESSED.

When we release all fear and doubt that we are being supported by a power higher than ourselves in the direction of our greatest good, we are calmer, more at peace, we have less frustrating thoughts running through our minds and we sleep better at night. We are at peace.

3. YOU FOCUS MORE ON THE PRESENT.

You know that your thoughts create your reality so you are intentionally aware of what you are thinking in the present moment and don't get sucked back into the past or out worrying about the future. You are focusing on the now.

4. YOU ARE CLEAR ABOUT WHAT YOU WANT IN LIFE.

You have crystal clear goals and because of this certainty the universe can more easily bring about your desire.

5. YOU FEEL HAPPIER.

The Law of Attraction works based on the intentions that you set, so if you emit positive energy and try your best every single day you will likely have a better sense of well being overall. If you have been feeling light hearted and free lately then the Law of Attraction is working for you.

6. YOU HAVE PEACE IN YOUR HEART.

7. GOOD THINGS KEEP COMING YOUR WAY.

While we all must face obstacles in our lives, you begin to notice more doors opening for you, you feel lighter, healthier and happier. You start to notice that the good in your life finally outshines the bad.

8. YOUR INTUITION IS AT AN ALL TIME HIGH.

You have an increased sense of knowing and you begin to understand what you need to become the master of your life. You move though life with ease and use your intuition to guide you along the way.

9. YOU'LL START TO NOTICE SIGNS THAT POINT TO YOUR SUCCESS.

You'll start noticing the right people coming into your life, you'll have better experiences and life will just seem to sync up for you with a series of synchronicities.

10. YOU HAVE MORE FINANCIAL SUCCESS.

When the Law of Attraction is working in your life, you'll notice more opportunities for financial abundance. You will finally get that business off the ground that you have been struggling with for quite some time. Anything is possible as long as you have the right intentions and never give up.

11. YOU BEGIN TO LIVE THE LIFE YOU'VE ALWAYS IMAGINED.

You will start manifesting your dreams and desires at a much faster rate. You focus your intentions on what you want and you hold that frequency until it materializes. As you create momentum, the universe will continue to bless you with more abundance.

The other thing I like to do is keep a "success journal" a log of evidence that the Law of Attraction is working in my life. Every night before I go to bed, I list all of my triumphs and successes for the day no matter how small they are, and I give thanks for them. When we give thanks to the universe the universe responds in delivering more things for us to be grateful for. It also works well with the "last 5 minute" principle, which allows me to absorb only good thoughts through out my sleep that sink into my subconscious, and I wake up feeling happy. Try it and make it a daily practice. It will transform your life.

Watch your words. Your mind believes everything you say.

#GirlWithAPlanBook

CHAPTER 30

WATCH YOUR WORDS

The majority of people sleepwalk through life and speak without thinking. We rarely stop to think about what we are saying. Remember when you were young and your parents used to say, think before you speak! They were right. Words have incredible power. They have the ability to create and the ability to destroy. The good news is we have a tongue, which we have full control over. It's up to us which words we choose to speak.

I want you to remember this sequence forever:

WORDS = THOUGHTS = FEELINGS = ACTIONS = RESULTS.

Let me explain this sequence. We are constantly talking to ourselves whether it's in our head or out loud. It is estimated that we have an average of 60,000 thoughts a day.

This is how the sequence goes: the words that we are telling ourselves, translate into the thoughts that we are having, whether consciously or subconsciously and most of the time unfortunately it's subconsciously. Those thoughts translate into feelings and our feelings determine the actions that we take in life. The actions show up as results. Those results can be positive or negative. We definitely know which one we are getting don't we?

So again let's go back:

Words = Thoughts = Feelings = Actions

Anytime you're getting a result that you are not happy with, go back to the beginning which all starts with the words you speak and think. Thoughts are words we say in our mind. Whether you're speaking the words out loud or holding them in, those words count. What are you saying to yourself? What are you telling yourself on a day-to-day basis, on an hour-to-hour basis? What are you telling yourself on a minute-to-minute basis?

Successful people are very aware of the words they are using at any given moment. They are master of their words and they choose them very carefully. They are consciously selective about what comes out of their mouths. They know that if they don't control their words, their words will control them.

Successful people understand that to be more effective, one needs to use words of positivity, encouragement, self-confidence and belief. They constantly are using words of affirmation, appreciation, gratitude, love, possibility and big dreams!

And they fully realize that whatever they speak, will manifest into their reality.

Unsuccessful people on the other hand use words that damage. They damage possibility, creation and vision. Their words stifle, block and prevent all that is good from coming to them.

A great book recommendation I have is the "Power of I AM" by Joel Osteen. He talks about whatever you put after the "I AM" you are inviting into your life. So, if you say things like: I am ugly, I am stupid, I am fat, I am old, I am wrinkled, that is exactly what comes looking for you! You are summoning that into your life. Be very careful with what you put after I AM because it's going to show up in your life!

Alternatively when you say things like: I AM capable, I am resourceful, I am powerful, I am vibrant, I am young, I am attractive, I am beautiful...all of that comes looking for you.

When we think about the words that we use on a daily basis, the words form our thoughts and when we hold a thought in our mind it translates into a certain feeling. Thoughts equal feelings. And, the way that we feel will always determine what actions we take in life. If we are feeling happy, if we are feeling excited, if we are feeling confident, if we are feeling capable and if we have the confidence that we know we can accomplish something then the action that we are going to take is going to be in line with that feeling and it's going to give us the result that we want.

For example, if I'm feeling happy and confident that I can launch something whether it's a new business, write a book, or pick up the phone and make a sales call, I'm going to take an action that is in alignment with that feeling.

On the other hand, If I'm telling myself words of defeat, lack and disbelief then I will take a different action, which will usually equate to no action!

So once again it all comes down to the words. Your words formulate your thoughts, your thoughts translate into your feelings, and your feelings determine the actions that you will take on a day to day basis. The actions that you take on a day-to-day basis equal the results that you are getting in your life. The results don't lie. You either have what you want or you don't.

If you always think about this simple formula then you can always answer the question WHY, and you have the power to change it by consciously changing your words.

Every thought we think and every word we speak is creating our reality. Our thoughts go out into the universe and are brought back to us as experience. Once you understand this concept and accept it, you can begin to deliberately attract and create what you want in your life. You also begin to understand and become aware of what you don't want in your life and how you are contributing.

Most people walk around not being aware of their thoughts and then wonder why they feel the way they do and why they are getting the results they are getting.

So here's the plan: Check in with your thoughts on an hourly basis. What are you thinking about? Ask yourself, do I want this thought to create my reality? If the answer is no, then you need to replace it with words and thoughts that WILL create what you desire.

Awareness is the key to transformation.

Once we become aware of our thought we have the power to change it to one that serves us and empowers us to move in the direction of our dreams.

If you remember only one thing from this book, let it be this: you create your thoughts by the words you choose to tell yourself whether out loud or subconsciously playing in the back of your mind. Your thoughts create your intentions and your intentions create your reality.

If you can grasp this concept, you will discover that you can have, be or do anything in life. Your potential is only limited by who you think you are or are not.

"IT'S NOT WHO WE THINK WE ARE THAT HOLDS US BACK, IT'S WHO WE THINK WE'RE NOT."

Remember the universe is listening to everything you say and everything you think. The universe is answering.

Watch your words. It's the most important tip I can give you to living a life of your dreams.

CHAPTER 31

START BEFORE YOU'RE READY

A little bit goes a long way.

When we first think about setting big goals and big dreams we get excited and can't wait to get started. Our enthusiasm makes us feel like we can accomplish anything. What happens though is that when we realize how big we've set our goal, panic starts to set in and our fears and doubts start shouting at us.

You can't do that! What the heck were you thinking! Are you crazy? You're NEVER going to accomplish that! What a fool you are. The list goes on.

I want you to know that these are normal thoughts to have and that the way you are going to get over them is ACTION. Action in spite of these doubts and fears.

ONE BITE AT A TIME

How do you eat an elephant? One bite at a time. I know this sounds silly because obviously we don't eat elephants but the point is that even when something is so BIG that you can't possibly imagine how you're going to accomplish it, just know that if you keep taking baby steps consistently every single day, you WILL get there.

A journey of a thousand miles starts with a single step.

START BEFORE YOU'RE READY!

Someday is not a day of the week last time I checked.

The biggest reason people put off starting their dream project or launching their business is that they don't feel ready.

My website is not ready, it doesn't look the way I want it to. I haven't lost the weight I want to, so I'm not going to start dating until I do. I don't know the right people so I don't feel comfortable going to networking events. I don't have the right coach, I don't have the time, I don't have the money, I don't have the resources, I don't know how, I'll start when the kids go off to school and on and on.

These are just a few of the many excuses I hear when talking to and coaching women in my She's in Biz Blueprint Course.

Wake up call!

You're never going to be ready. You need to start before you're ready. Start. Why? Because when you begin something and you take an action, it creates momentum and you get unstuck. So just take a step, it doesn't have to be a big step. Take a small step. Take a tiny step, a baby step. Take it in spite of your legs shaking, and your knees wobbling and your palms sweating. Just take it.

And you know what happens when you do? Two things. First, you'll gain confidence to take the next step and the next step will appear for you.

Done is always better than perfect.

Movement creates energy and energy is necessary to create change. You've heard the expression nothing changes until you do.

Nothing is perfect. Perfect is just the way it is and just the way it's not. That's perfect. Perfect is exactly where you are today. That's perfect. You're perfect. Just the way you are. So stop trying to attain perfection, realize that you already have it right where you are.

Today is the perfect moment to be right where you are reading this very line in my book.

"Do what you can, with what you have, where you are." - Theodore Roosevelt

CHAPTER 32

FEAR IS A BAD MAN

What if I told you I know who is stopping you from living your dream? What if I told you I know his name and I know exactly where he lives.

Would you want to know the address so you could go and give him a big punch in the face?

Well I'll tell you his name. His name is FEAR. He lives in your mind. He takes up space inside your head. Stop being his landlord and kick him out. He is the one responsible for you not living your dreams. He is the one who is holding you back. Cutting you off from the life that you are capable of living. Starving you of possibility and creativity, and magic.

He's nasty right? So why are you letting him stay with you?

I created the Ladies WHO Lunch® Network to inspire women to be fearless and fabulous by helping them to realize and live their dream. I've interviewed a lot of them around what it means to be "fearless."

The answers might shock you. We are ALL scared to do something that we've never done before. We all experience fear. But, here's the catch.

Successful people feel the fear and do it anyways. They do it with sweaty palms. In my case with sweaty armpits, a dry mouth, wobbly knees, heart pounding, legs shaking, blood draining out of face feeling. There you have it, it's no big secret, even the most successful people feel FEAR but the difference is that they TAKE ACTION in spite of it.

Action is the antidote to fear.

When you take action you build up your courage, and the more times you build up your courage you become more confident and feel it less. I don't believe it ever truly goes away. When we are pushing ourselves out of our comfort zones no matter how successful we are to try different things, we will experience the butterflies in our stomach, light headed, heart pounding feeling of fear but if we learn to acknowledge these feelings as nothing more than physical sensations and take action despite them, they will subside and have less and less power over us the more that we do the thing that we fear....

Too many of us are not living our dreams because we are too busy living our fears.

Everything you've ever wanted is on the other side of FEAR.

Here's a tip I like to use every time I'm scared or nervous. I take the FEAR that I'm experiencing and I call it EXCITEMENT!

I remember waiting to take the stage to speak as the first speaker in front of 600 people at the inaugural SHE TALKS YVR in 2015. Someone asked me right before I was about to go on "Maria! are you nervous?" My answer, sweaty armpits, wobbly knees, whole body vibrating, heart-pounding answer was: NO! I'm EXCITED!"

If you think about it, the sensations that we experience when we are fearlful and when we are excited are essentially the same. We get butterflies in our stomach, our heart beats faster, and we feel more alive and alert. If we rename these emotions and call them excitement rather than fear, we would have an entirely different interpretation of what these sensations mean!

LWL member Laurie Ashley introduced me to a unique word that I love: nervocited. It's the feeling we get when we are excited and nervous at the same time, but when we use it, rather than conjuring negative connotations and keeping us stuck and paralyzed, it makes us feel giddy and excited. We use the word nervocited often and it helps us reframe the experience of feeling scared to one of excitement and aliveness which are not bad feelings to be experiencing last time I checked!

If you take all those feelings that you have when you're scared and re-name them and call them EXCITEMENT, then excitement becomes your new best friend, and we love it when EXCITEMENT comes to stay with us. She can stay with us as long as she likes.

CHAPTER 33

GET ON IT GIRL

Do you know the biggest dream killer out there?

PROSCRASTINATION.

It's a place dreams go to die. The key characteristic of all girls with a plan is the ability to execute at a quick speed. The more you think about something, the longer it takes to execute and often times doesn't happen at all.

Think about the last time you had to get into a swimming pool, you knew the water was going to be a little cold initially. But the longer you wait and stare at the cold water, the harder it is to get in because your fear has taken over your thoughts. Just jump! Stop thinking about it so much! The more you think, the more you stall, the more pain you are causing yourself unnecessarily.

Successful people are action takers. Doers. Risk takers. Implementation freaks!

Thinking about something is never going to make it happen. Taking action gets the ball rolling and sets everything in motion.

So why do we procrastinate so much? It's because we think we have time. We're constantly living in this state of "I'll get to that tomorrow" or "next week", "not now", and "I just don't have the time right now".

"We all have the same amount of time. The difference is what we choose to do with it."

The prescription is action.

"WE ALL HAVE DREAMS. THE ONLY DIFFERENCE BETWEEN THOSE WHO ACHIEVE THEIR DREAMS AND THOSE WHO DON'T IS THE ACTION THEY DO OR DON'T TAKE." – PETER LEGGE

Ideas without action are useless. Knowledge without implementation will get you nowhere.

It's in the doing, not the knowing where change happens and growth appears.

Have you ever met those people that have read a ton of books but fail to take any of the advice or implement anything that they have learned in the books?

You might be asking, well if action is the prescription for achieving our goals and dreams then why don't people take the necessary action needed to live their dream?

Here are some of my theories:

1. They are overwhelmed by their dream and have no idea what actions to take to get there. This is completely normal and to be expected. All those that started with a big dream had no idea how they were going to accomplish it.

When we have a dream, particularly a big dream, we won't know how everything is going to unfold. What we do need to know is that we have to take the first step. Whatever that looks like and however small or insignificant you think that might be. Just take the first step, when you do that the next step appears, and the next, and so on and so on.

2. They believe wishing is the same as doing. We've all heard that a dream without a definite plan or a deadline is merely a wish. Don't spend your life wishing and hoping. These are the two wasted emotions that will get you nowhere fast. Don't wish, do! Don't hope, have faith and trust instead. There is a misconception about the Law of Attraction. It's that people think they can wish something into being without taking any steps to make it happen! Wrong. Besides having a strong belief the universe will bring us what we ask for, we also need to take the action and do the hard work to back that belief.

3. They don't believe in themselves. This stops the majority of people. It's human tendency to think we are not qualified to be, do or have what we want. Our belief by nature is that someone else has more right than we do. When I ask women why they aren't living their dream, they often answer with one of many excuses. "I just don't have the time", "I don't have the skills", "I don't know HOW", "I don't have the money", this list is endless.

My answer is always this. If it's a priority, you will find the time, the skills, the know how, the money. The resourcefulness of a girl with a plan is also endless.

"YOUR PRIORITIES ARE NOT WHAT YOU SAY THEY ARE, THEY ARE WHAT YOU DO."

We always find the time and resources to do the things that are important to us. The things that we consider priorities. Just take a look at your day. I challenge you to carry around a notebook and for the whole day, every hour, document what activities you are carrying out. You will quickly see where your priorities are.

4. They think they have TIME so they procrastinate. Our time on this earth has a limit. Yet, many people fail to take this into account on a daily basis. They keep thinking that there will always be time, or that they can start tomorrow. Tomorrow becomes next week, and then next week becomes next month, next month turns into one year. Before they know it they are at the end of their life, with their dreams still inside them. Someday is not a day of the week as Brian Tracy tells

us. We cannot hope and wish to live out our dreams someday. The time to take action is now. The power is in the present moment. Everything you do on a daily basis is contributing to your future. Think about that. Are the activities and actions you take on a daily basis in alignment with what you say you want to achieve? If not, change them immediately, and get going.

Here are some tips to avoid procrastination:

There's something you have to get done. It's been on your to-do list for a while, but you just haven't gotten around to it. With your busy schedule and competing priorities, there is always something more urgent to work on and the truth is that it's a difficult task. So what do you do? If you're like most of us, you continue to avoid it until the last possible moment and then end up doing a rushed job.

> *Opportunity is like music. You hear the music but you still have to decide and get up and dance.*

Hopefully, it's passable, but definitely it will not be your best work. Procrastination can significantly limit the potential of both you and your business. It might be costing you more than you realize. Here are some tips that will help you break this bad habit:

DECIDE ON YOUR PRIORITIES.

What do you need to get done right now? Choose one or two tasks that are your top priority and don't do anything else until they are complete. If another urgent task comes up, you can move it to your top priority or put it aside until you finish your first task. The key is to be deliberate about how you are spending your time.

BREAK IT DOWN INTO STEPS.

When there is a big job to do, many of us get overwhelmed and avoid it completely. You may find that it helps to break the job down into steps, and to focus on one task at a time. You can even tell yourself that you will work on the task for ten minutes and then you'll take a break. Often the toughest part is getting started.

ELIMINATE DISTRACTIONS.

What are your favourite time wasters? Social media? Video games? Talking on the telephone? Television? We all have a resident time thief and chances are you know what yours is. Remove the temptation by turning off your phone, television, computer, and whatever else your vice is.

APPROACH IT IN A DIFFERENT WAY.

If you're finding it difficult to get started, it might help you to work on a different part of the task. For example, if you're writing a report, could you start by doing research, or planning the outline? Sometimes when you approach a task in a different way, it feels less overwhelming.

STAY FOCUSED ON YOUR GOALS.

Why is this task your biggest priority? What will this task do for your business? Reminding yourself why you are doing all of this is helpful because it keeps your attention on your goals and reminds you how the work you are doing today will help you achieve them.

When we procrastinate, we are essentially burying our head in the sand and hoping that the difficult task will just go away. It won't and putting it off only makes it harder. You may have to force yourself to get started, but once you're engaged with it, you will find that it's easier than you thought. If you can successfully overcome procrastination, it will significantly contribute to your productivity and success.

You'll never get anywhere standing still.

Commitment means staying loyal to what you said you were going to do long after the mood you said it in has left you.

#GirlWithAPlanBook

CHAPTER 34

MOTIVATION IS A LIAR

The thing about motivation is that people wait until they feel motivated to do something and most of the time unfortunately we are not going to feel like doing what is good for us in order to move along in our journey. This is just a simple fact.

We know that running is good for us, we know that going to the gym is good for us, we know that reading is good for us, we know that eating healthy is good for us but yet we don't do it. And the problem is that we wait until we feel like doing it, until we get that feeling of ok now I want to do it, and then we do it.

But the point is, motivation is a liar. You'll never really feel like it. I say PUSH YOURSELF. Push yourself to get your running shoes on and get out the door, don't even think about it. A great book that I recommend is "The 5 Second Rule" by Mel Robbins. Her method is simple. She counts backwards from 5 to 0 ...5, 4, 3, 2, 1, and then she physically moves. She gets her body into ACTION.

The act of physically moving is actually going to propel you to take a different action whether you feel like it or not, and then she does the what's required. Whether that's going for a run, writing, making a call, scheduling an appointment, answering an email.

Whatever it is that you need to do, you need to PUSH YOURSELF. Why? Because I promise you, you are not going to feel like it 24/7. Yes, there are going to be days that you feel more motivated than others, but the key to success is pushing through those times when you lack the motivation. I guarantee that it's normal not to feel motivated all the time. It's the way our bodies function best. Our body and our mind want to be comfortable. That is the nature of the human disposition. We don't want to go to a place of discomfort, but what we don't realize is that going to that place of discomfort is the only way that we are going to transform and see any kind of change in our lives.

I was at yoga, I looked up and noticed a poster just before heading into the changing room that read: The only way to GROW is to STRETCH.

Going to a place of discomfort is never comfortable, it's not easy and you don't feel motivated to do so, but you need to push yourself. Don't worry about feeling motivated or think there's something wrong with you if you don't feel motivated. Give yourself the push to just do what needs to be done.

What happens when you actually start doing the things that need to be done to move you forward, is you're going to start creating something called MOMENTUM. Once you push yourself to do something that you didn't feel like doing, and you actually get it done, you feel really good about yourself and you say hey, that wasn't so bad. That momentum propels you to keep going to do the next thing, and the next thing, and the next thing.

I believe motivation is a habit that you have to cultivate. Don't worry when you don't feel motivated. Push yourself to take an action forward and then the motivation will come.

"COMMITMENT IS SAYING YOU'LL DO THE THING YOU WERE GOING TO DO LONG AFTER THE FEELING YOU SAID IT IN HAS LEFT YOU."

When you learn how much you're worth, you'll stop giving people discounts.

#GirlWithAPlanBook

CHAPTER 35

SAY NO TO MAKE ROOM FOR YES

Say YES to only the things that will bring you closer to your goals. This is very important because as most of us are passionate entrepreneurs with a lot of energy and a lot of ideas, we will often have a lot of opportunities that come our way or will be presented to us.

I always like to remind myself to say NO to make room for YES. Stay focused on where you want to go and ask yourself does saying yes to this bring me any closer to my goal? If yes, then do it, if not then scrap it!

I remember in the beginning of my career I would say YES to absolutely EVERYTHING for fear that I might be missing out on something important! But now I've really learned to try to narrow my focus to those activities, situations and people who are aligned with my goals and where it is that I want to go.

Because I tend to get off track quite a bit, yes, even to this day, here's how I keep myself focused and how you can too!

Here's the plan to stay focused.

In my smart phone in my notes section I write my top 5 priorities for the year, I call them my 5 points of focus. And I look at them EACH DAY. Yes, it's that important for me to always keep bringing my focus back to what it is that I want to achieve. Each time I'm asked to participate in something I will take a quick sneak peek at this list and if the activity or project has nothing to do with what's on that list, guess what my answer is?

One of the reasons so many entrepreneurs burn out and lose focus is because of this. They take their focus away from the things that matter to do things that don't matter. Activities that have little or no impact on what it is they are trying to achieve. They often feel like they are pulled in a million different directions, kind of like a chicken with their head cut off running from task to task without any real sense of direction. Don't let this happen to you.

Someone who is focused on where they are going makes decisions easily.

Here's the question to keep you on track: Is what I'm doing right now helping me achieve my goals and my priorities?

CHAPTER 36

HOW TO STAY FOCUSED

Developing clarity and focus will determine how your life will turn out. Whatever you give your attention, energy and focus to, you will receive more of in your life whether positive or negative. Lack of focus will prevent you from living the life you dream of.

Don't waste the most valuable resource you have. Time. Here's how to stay focused on your purpose and what it is you want to achieve in life:

She remembered who she was and the game changed.

Here's the plan to follow.

1. ASK YOURSELF WHAT IS MY PERSONAL MISSION IN LIFE?

What is it that I want to accomplish, what message do I want to share with the world? I always ask people when I interview them for LunchWithMaria TV (www.LunchWithMaria.com), "If I gave you a microphone and you could speak to the whole world, what would you want to say to them in one sentence?" When you are really clear on what your mission in life is, the things that don't matter will distract you less, and you will turn down opportunities that don't align with your mission.

Your attention will be diverted and diluted if you do not have a clear mission. My mission is to inspire women to be fearless and fabulous by helping them realize and live their dream. Everything I do stems from that mission, and speaks back to it, including writing Girl With A Plan.

2. GET RID OF DISTRACTIONS.

Distractions will kill your dreams. If you're going on Facebook, make sure you limit your time to 10 or 15 minutes. Set a timer and then when that timer goes off, get back to work! I also like to turn my phone off and all the notifications to silent if I'm working on something where I don't want to be interrupted.

3. REALIZE HOW VALUABLE YOUR TIME IS.

It is something you'll never get back. Keep an agenda of your day. What do you need to get done today in order to move you to where you want to be tomorrow? Make a list. Stick to the list. Start with the hardest task first. Get it out of the way. Make sure your to-do list is in line with your personal mission.

4. REMEMBER TO TAKE BREAKS.

No one is expected to work 8 hours straight without taking a break, nor should they. Reward yourself by taking small breaks after accomplishing a task. Sometimes I find a refreshing walk around the block helps to clear my energy and revitalize me giving me the juice I need to go on.

Stop being distracted by things that have nothing to do with your goal.

#GirlWithAPlanBook

CHAPTER 37

SHINY OBJECT SYNDROME

Have you heard of Shiny Object Syndrome?

By definition it's the attraction to objects that exhibit a glassy, polished, gleaming or otherwise **shiny** appearance. Something as simple as a reflection in your peripheral vision may easily distract your attention.

Fortunately, it's not a diagnosable affliction, but it can make you take your business down the wrong path and put a huge halt on the realization of your dream. How do you know if you have it and how can you get rid of it?

Here's the plan:

First answer these questions to see if in fact you suffer from this syndrome:

1. Do you often feel like the day has just flown by but you really haven't accomplished anything?

2. Are you easily bored and have a hard time focusing on one thing at a time?

3. Do you find yourself starting something then switching to something completely new before finishing the initial thing that you set out to do?

4. Do you feel yourself saying YES to a lot of things then feeling completely overwhelmed, confused and stressed?

5. Are you a generally an impatient person?

6. Are you often sucked in by social media only to find out that 2 hours have passed and you haven't accomplished anything on your to-do list?

If you answered yes to 2 or more of these questions then most likely you are a sufferer.

Essentially shiny object syndrome (SOS) is a disease of distraction, and it affects entrepreneurs specifically because of the qualities that make them unique.

Entrepreneurs tend to be highly motivated. We love starting new projects and creating new things. We are multi-passionate by nature!

Normally, these are great characteristics to have, but when SOS sets in, it forces you to chase project after project, and change after change, never settling on one specific thing long enough for the time it takes to make it successful.

It's called shiny object syndrome because it's the entrepreneurial equivalent of a small child chasing after shiny objects. Once they play with the toy for a while they immediately lose interest and start chasing the next thing.

For entrepreneurs, rather than literal shiny objects or toys, our distractions may be new business objectives, marketing strategies, working with a different kind of client or even other business ventures.

Shiny Object Syndrome will kill your chances of fully living your dream as your energy will be dispersed and depleted, because shifting your focus can not only be very draining but highly ineffective!

Here are 5 tips to avoid getting sucked in by SOS and to stop being distracted by what's not moving you forward! These tips will help you get really intentional about your goals and will help you stop being distracted by all the shiny things!

1. Start every day by being intentional. That means I write down what my intentions for that day are. I'm specific about these and stay on top of them. I have them written out in a notebook very clearly defined. I write them down the night before and then keep them where I can SEE them while I'm working and going about the day. I Look at them often, ask, "is what i'm doing right now a reflection of my intention for

this day?" If the answer is NO, I scrap it and get back to being intentional about my activity and time.

> *"BE A MEANINGFUL SPECIFIC RATHER THAN A WONDERING GENERALITY." – BRIAN TRACY*

2. Focus on one thing at a time and avoid multi-tasking! Those people who start on one task and stick with it until they are complete achieve the most success rather than jumping from task to task or trying to do more than one thing at one. This is called multi-tasking and although you might think you are being more productive, truth is it has just the opposite effect as research has shown. People who multi-task get a lot less done than those who focus on doing one thing at a time from start to finish.

3. Don't let social media get the best of you! Limit your time on Facebook, Instagram, Pinterest, Youtube or whatever your choice of social media drug is. Why? Because if you don't you will easily be pulled into the black hole of browser blackout. This means that what you intended to only be a short break on social turned into two hours later. Don't let your day get away on you like this.

4. Being busy does not mean being productive! In getting ahead and when it comes to achieving your goals, it's all about RESULTS! Focus on the tasks that are actually going to make a difference and move you forward. We often feel busy but when asked what we truly accomplished on any given day, the result can be dismal.

5. Use a timer to keep you on track. A timer can keep us accountable, whether it's limiting our time on social media or keeping us focused on a particular task to move us forward in our business. When you know you only have a set amount of time to accomplish things in, you tend to work faster and not waste any of it!

I like to use the Pomodoro Technique.

The Pomodoro Technique is a proven and popular time management life hack that will help you to be more productive in less time, and let's face it, isn't that what we all want?

The main idea with the technique is to work in blocks of time, typically 25 minutes. These are called Pomodoro Sessions, followed by a 5-minute break. Each session should demand your full attention on one task, this means absolutely no moving around from task to task and every break requires you to step away from your work to rest.

The result has greatly improved productivity during focused work sessions that can be maintained through effectively managing distractions and taking regular breaks. Many successful people use this technique and swear by it, why not give it a try?

6. Sit on ideas before launching them. Before you begin work on that new project that's going to make "a huge difference", take a moment and really think about it. I do this when I go shopping. When I see something in a store that I immediately fall in love with but that is perhaps too

expensive or something that I don't "need" I give myself two days to sleep on it and if I am still thinking about it and can't get it out of my head then I go back and buy it. Guess what happens? The majority of the time, I don't go back.

It takes time to build a business and reach your goals and dreams. It is not something that happens overnight and it is definitely not something that will happen by switching your precious energy from idea to idea. Focus on doing one thing at a time and doing it really well before moving on to anything else.

Stop being distracted by things that have nothing to do with your goals.

CHAPTER 38

CHASING RABBITS

I learned a technique from Gary Keller in his book called "The ONE Thing" which changed my life and my business significantly, and gave me more clarity, less stress and made me a heck of a lot productive. It's called Time Blocking.

Most people who work for themselves wake up and have no idea what to do. They feel scattered and overwhelmed because there is so much to be done. They don't have a schedule and they have no idea what their day will look like. This is not the Girl With A Plan. The Girl With A Plan knows that time blocking is her best friend.

Time Blocking is setting aside time to work on the most important thing in your business that can only be done by you. When it's done, it makes everything else unnecessary or easier.

If you're in real estate for example the most important thing is to generate leads and then to effectively follow up on the leads and convert them into paying customers. This is your ONE thing. This thing has to get done and get done consistently otherwise you're no longer in business.

So how does this one thing get done? For most of us, it gets done sometimes, maybe on days that we feel like it, or when we have a few hours here and there, or when we run out of leads and our funnel has dried up and we begin to panic so we start making some calls. In other words, our ONE thing becomes random and haphazard creating random and haphazard results.

Top producers and high achieving individuals always make the time to execute and work on their most important task in order to reach their goal. As Gary Keller calls it, "their ONE thing". It's up to you to discover what that one thing is in your business, and once you do, you must protect it with your life and make it a priority.

So how do you do that? You actually take out your calendar and block off chunks of time during which you will work on that ONE thing. It may be every day for 2 hours between 9am to 11am, or it may be every Tuesday and Thursdays from 2 to 4pm. Whatever you decide, make sure it works for you.

This time is sacred, uninterrupted time. This means doing anything else other than your ONE thing during this time is out of the question. You don't check emails, look at your phone, answer calls, or work on any other project. Adding those during this block is called multi-tasking and does not work!

You cannot possibly be effective or efficient when you try to do more than one thing at a time. Multi-tasking just like motivation is a liar. It is NOT the way to get ahead, in fact studies have shown time and time again that those that multi task are actually less productive than those that focus and work on one task at a time without interruptions.

When we multitask we are essentially distracted. Our attention is spread thin and the things that we are working on don't get the focus that they deserve. One thing at a time is always your best bet. Work on one task uninterrupted and finish it, then move on to the next.

Think of time blocking as an appointment with yourself. In business, you would not miss an appointment with a customer or a potential client or a business associate so why would you miss the most important appointment of all? Why would you miss the appointment with yourself? Understanding this concept will drastically alter the course of your life and the results you see in your business. When you keep the appointment with yourself you are showing respect for yourself, you are showing love for yourself, you are radiating self-confidence and you are setting up boundaries that will not be stepped on.

> *If you chase two rabbits, you will not catch either one.*
> RUSSIAN PROVERB

This self-confidence allows you to move freely and effortlessly through life, because protecting our time is the most crucial thing you can do. Our time is valuable and it is the thing that if used correctly will get us to our goals and dreams. Don't throw your time around like it means nothing. Give it the respect it deserves. Use it wisely and it will work for you.

Let people know that when you are time blocking that you cannot and will not be interrupted. At first people may try to take advantage of your limits but don't let them, stay firm and keep the appointment with yourself. Refuse to be interrupted, refuse to take phone calls and answer text message and emails during this time. Soon it will become a habit and as we know by now, habits are the foundations for success.

According to research it takes about 66 days to form a habit. Don't be discouraged, keep going, keep practicing your time blocking until it becomes so engrained into your daily routine that it no longer feels onerous but rather easy and effortless. Want to know the best part? The results that you will experience will be phenomenal and this will give you the momentum to keep going.

Keep the appointment with yourself and then schedule everything else around that. You will feel less resentful of others and the demands on your time because your most important task will have already been done.

It's also important to Time Block your vacations. So just as important as it is to Time Block your most important thing, remember to schedule time off to re-charge and re-energize so that you can be more effective during the time that you are working.

Nobody should work all the time nor is it healthy or productive. Everyone needs downtime. It's vital to maximum productivity. You cannot be successful or productive if you're tired, and burnt out. Remember to Time Block your off time as well!

Your most important meeting is the one you keep with yourself, make it your priority.

Is what you're doing right now bringing you closer or further away from your goal?

#GirlWithAPlanBook

CHAPTER 39

IS IT A DMA OR A TW?

The only reason you don't have what you want yet is because you're focused on Time Wasters (TWs) rather than Difference Making Activities (DMAs).

That's really the truth. Hate to be so blunt. Success is directly related to the actions you take on a daily, hourly and minute-by-minute basis. If you're not seeing the results you want, it's because you're not doing the DMA that is needed to yield these results. Simple. Not easy.

What exactly is a DMA? A DMA is what I like to call a Difference Making Activity. This is something that when done will have a direct effect in moving your business or whatever other goal you want to accomplish forward.

What are examples of DMAs? Calling a client, sending an email to a prospect, going to the gym, writing a few pages in your book, creating content for your blog, writing out your goals.

These are all activities that if done, will move you forward in some way.

On the other hand, TWs are the time-wasting activities. These are the easy ones because they tend to be fun.

Examples of time wasters: when you're stuck in the scrolling loop on social media. Talking aimlessly to friends on the phone because you're trying to avoid your work, worrying about things that you've no control over, browsing shopping sites, daydreaming. TWs are the things that waste your time.

Being busy does not equal being productive. You could be busy all day long and not get a single thing done. Productive is where it's at. Productive is what we need to strive for if we are to attain our dream.

How do we become more productive? Well first off saying yes to the DMAs that are in alignment with our goals and NO to the TWs that have nothing to do with our goals!

Here's a simple daily practice that will help you stay focused on DMAs. Every night before I go to bed I list my most important tasks for the following day. When I awake I am ready to go and I'm not scrambling trying to figure out what the heck I'm supposed to be doing that day!

I then prioritize which task needs to get done first. And remember, the task that often needs to get done first is usually the one that we don't want to do! It is important to get this task done as soon as possible. Why? Because once we finish it, we have a sense of accomplishment and we created momentum to go on to the rest of the tasks with greater confidence. Do what needs to be done first.

This is the system loosely adopted from Brian Tracy in his book "Eat That Frog"

A task - something that NEEDS to get done and if not done will have great consequences on your business. (Only YOU can do these tasks)

B task - something you must do but has mild consequences if you don't do it (never do a B task when an A task has not been completed)

C task - something that would be nice to do, but has NO consequences if not done (having coffee with a friend)

D task - something that can be delegated to someone else like a VA, this is something you want to do because you're probably a control freak like me, but shouldn't do so that you can free up your time to focus on the A tasks that only YOU can do.

E task - something you need to eliminate all together as it makes no difference to your business.

If you apply this ABCDE method on a daily list to your activities your results will be nothing less than astounding.

To help you understand the impact of DMAs, let's look at the 80/20 rule also known as the "Pareto Principle". It basically states that 20 percent of your activities will account for 80 percent of your results. In other words 20 percent of your tasks will account for 80 percent of the value of what you do. So, if you have a list of 10 to do items, 2 of these items will turn out to be worth 5 or 10 times more than the other 8 items put together.

The unfortunate part is that most people tend to procrastinate on the items that are the most valuable. Instead they busy themselves with the trivial TWs. These TWs have no impact on their business and life.

Your time and energy are the most valuable assets you have, once you spend them, you can't get them back.

The most valuable tasks that you should accomplish each day are often the hardest to get through but keep in mind they are the ones that will yield you the most results and rewards. Keep saying no to the TWs and keep focusing on the DMAs. It does get easier with practice, and soon you will identify the difference between a DMA and a TW and know which one is best for you at any given time.

Resist the temptation to be distracted by TWs. Focus on the DMAs, and always be asking yourself this question on a consistent basis: Is this a DMA or a TW?

It really is the question that will shape your future and change your life.

CHAPTER 40

ENERGY VAMPIRES

Your time and your energy are the two most precious commodities you OWN.

They are invaluable. Both of them are limited. We only have a certain amount of time in the day, we only have a certain amount of time on this planet. The same goes for our energy. Once we give it away we are depleted.

Stop giving your precious time and energy to people who don't deserve it. People who after being with them you feel drained, and depleted then you have nothing left to focus on you, your goals and your dreams.

Walk away from the energy suckers, and what I like to call the energy vampires that leave you feeling lifeless and powerless after each encounter with them.

If you are going to move forward and be that girl with a plan, then you need to ditch these people ASAP!

So, you're probably thinking ok well what if it's my family?

Spend less time with them and realize that it's not your job to fix or try to change everyone it's theirs. Your job is to focus on improving yourself. YOU will be the best and most rewarding project you will ever work on.

CHAPTER 41

THE POWER OF ASSOCIATION

There's an expression in Greek, and it probably doesn't translate very well, but it goes something like this: Show me who your friends are, and I will tell you who you are. When I was young I grew up with a lot of these sayings, often relayed to me by my Dad who would repeat them over and over to me until they were imprinted into my mind for good. This one really stuck with me though.

Someone once said that the person you become in 5 years, will be determined by the people you meet, and the books you've read. Anyone that knows me, knows I'm a huge bookworm. I've taken the advice of my mentor Dr. Peter Legge who consistently reads 1 book a week.

It is clear to me that successful people are constantly learning and they do it by reading and always improving themselves.

Let's talk about how the people you choose to associate with can have a powerful influence on your life and your future.

Your associations will nudge you slightly over time. You may not realize the effect they are having on your life, but it's there I promise you. Think about it as if you were on a life raft and the current was pushing you ever so slightly along, you may not notice any big changes, but one day you will find yourself in the middle of the ocean and wonder how you got there! You won't realize how far they've nudged you in a particular direction. This is how extremely powerful your associations can be!

"YOU ARE THE AVERAGE OF THE 5 PEOPLE THAT YOU ASSOCIATE WITH THE MOST." - JIM ROHN

What does this mean exactly? It means that you will have the average combined attitude of these people, behaviours, and habits (whether good or bad). Their lifestyle, the books they read, even their combined income!

Who we spend our time with dictates what conversations we have, what thoughts and beliefs we entertain, what habits and opinions we are exposed to. Eventually if we spend enough time with these people, we will start to act like they act, talk like they talk, and think like they think.

One of my favourite expressions is "You can't expect to put your hand in a jar of honey, pull it out and then not expect anything to stick to it!"

Unfortunately, when people are not living their dream, it's because they are not associating with the right people to help them get there. Often times our associations are made unconsciously, without really thinking about who it is that we are allowing into our life and why. It's only by becoming very conscious of who we let into our lives that we gain our power.

Surround yourself with people who see the greatness in you even when you don't see it yourself.

You might be thinking well I can hang out with some people, but I'm not going to be like them, their behaviour will not affect me. Nothing is further from the truth. Everything affects you. Every word they say, every move they make, you are constantly absorbing whether at a conscious or subconscious level. It's the subconscious level that is even scarier because we know that the subconscious mind is where all the power is held.

Have you ever hung out with a group of people who are health conscious and been out to a restaurant with them? Do you find yourself making different choices based on their selection? The reverse is also true. Bad habits rub off easily, so do good ones.

You will eventually mimic the behaviour of those that surround you. You will match their attitudes, perspectives, mindset, beliefs, and even earning potential! In a study conducted at Harvard, it was found that your reference group (the people you spend the most time with) will determine up to 90% of your success or failure in life. It went on to reveal that your choice of reference group is more important in determining your success or failure in life than anything else!

> *"IF YOU WANT TO FLY WITH EAGLES, YOU CAN'T CONTINUE TO SURROUND YOURSELF WITH PIGEONS."*

I wish I had actively practiced this philosophy throughout my 20s and 30s more than I did, however it's never too late. Start where you are. Start now. When I created the Ladies WHO Lunch® Network, I wanted to immerse myself and give others an opportunity to put themselves in an environment of success. To learn more about how who you surround yourself with can make all the difference, visit www.LWLNetwork.com to receive a personal and exclusive invitation from me to join this transformational community of goal getters. You have nothing to lose and everything to gain.

> *"SURROUND YOURSELF WITH PEOPLE WHO INSPIRE YOU AND MOTIVATE YOU. PART OF LOVING YOURSELF IS HAVING A HIGH STANDARD FOR YOUR INNER CIRCLE."*

Here's how to evaluate all your associations and put them into one of 3 categories:

1. There are some people that you will need to disassociate with and break away from completely because the cost of having them in your life is too great. I know that this is not easy but I do believe that once you make room for the people that should be in your life, then the ones who shouldn't easily

slip away. Once you let go of associations that do not serve your highest good, you then create space for those that do. The effect of the wrong exposure to certain people is so detrimental to your success. Ask yourself how much your success means to you. You can use an affirmation that I recite daily, place it on a cue card and repeat it until it is imprinted into your subconscious: "I am allowing what no longer serves my highest good to peacefully dissolve and effortlessly melt away. I am free."

2. There's another category that should be under the title "Limited Associations" this could be a family member that is constantly negative and always telling you that your dream or aspirations are too big. You want to limit your time with these people and although you may love them, you don't need to spend 24/7 with them.

3. Find people who have been where you want to go! This is the fun part. Now I realize that sometimes you may not be able to reach these people in person, and that's ok. I have a lot of online mentors who I "spend" a lot of time with, whether it's listening to an inspirational recording or an impactful podcast. However it's also important to seek these individuals out in person too! Find someone who has already accomplished what it is you wish to achieve in whatever area of your life you want to work on. Spend more time with these people! How you might ask? Join a networking group, a professional association, go to a meet up or form your own mastermind group of like minded individuals and meet on a regular basis. This can be live or online or a combination of both. Find where these people congregate and then go and

make friends. If you are a female entrepreneur looking to build valuable connections we look forward to meeting you at www.LWLNetwork.com.

I tell women before they join our group that they will meet someone in the network that will change their life. Yes, that's how dramatic I am, but it's also how strongly I believe in the power of association.

> *"BE CAREFUL WHOM YOU ASSOCIATE WITH. IT IS HUMAN TO IMITATE THE HABITS OF THOSE WITH WHOM WE INTERACT." – EPICTETUS, ANCIENT GREEK PHILOSOPHER.*

CHAPTER 42

MONKEY SEE, MONKEY DO

As parents, why are we so worried about who our kids hang out with? Because we know that if they get in with the wrong crowd they can be easily influenced to make bad decisions that will affect their future!

We are protective of our children and the company they keep and rightly so. You are a product of your environment. When kids are little they tend to imitate and copy the actions of those around them. As adults, we do the same.

What do I mean by this? I mean you are the average of those people you associate with most. You are the average of their income, their belief system, their education, and their ultimate level of success. Their level of success will dictate your level of success.

That's why people say that success leaves clues. If you want to attain a certain level of success you need to model someone who has achieved and attained what you want. This model will take you where you want to go.

If you want to know what your future will be, just look at the last 5 conversations you had.

Who were the conversations with? What did you speak about? Did these conversations in any way shape or form contribute to your future and to getting you closer to your goals and dreams?

Who are you spending your valuable time with on a daily basis?

Who you spend time with is who you become.

Successful people know that if they are the smartest person in the room, they are in the wrong room!

Do you want to spend time with people who earn $20,000 a year or would you rather spend time with someone earning $1,000,000 if this scenario were true? I know what my choice would be.

David Foster, an award winning Grammy producer and philanthropist who has produced names like Celine Dion, Whitney Houston, Michael Buble, Barbara Streisand and many more was asked a question. He was asked a very important question.

The question was, what is the secret to success in ONE WORD? He surveyed the audience and I remember hearing answers like:

Money! Passion! Hard work! Perseverance! Patience! David said NOOOOO not any of these.

The secret to success in one word he said is: NETWORKING.

It's who you surround yourself with. It's who you are learning from.

Think of life like a game of tennis.

In order to play the game, we need a partner. If you are playing with someone that is at your level, you might have fun and you might be comfortable but you will never improve because they have nothing new to teach you.

If you play with someone at the same level as you there is no growth, no progress. You both know the same skill set. You have nothing new to learn from each other.

Your goal should be to get in the game with someone a little better than you. Someone you can learn from, someone who has something to teach you. Someone who has a skill that you lack which is necessary for your success.

These are the people you want to surround yourself with in life. The people that inspire you, the people that have gone to places you want to go to, the people that have achieved results that you only dream of right now. These will be the game changers for you. These are the ones that will cause you to move to a different level. These are the ones to help you grow, to transform, and to ultimately get you closer to your dream.

Take a step back and look at your life and who's in it. Who are you spending your time with? Is it people who will take you higher or those who will keep you stuck? Take inventory daily. Our lives will imitate the people we surround ourselves with. Hence the expression, monkey see, monkey do.

It's important to remember the players that are not as good as you too. It's ok to play with these players once in a while because it is through serving others and giving back and sharing what we've learned that ultimately fulfills us even more than the success that we have achieved.

Don't forget to pull someone up as you rise. Think of it as a ladder. As you reach your hand up to someone, remember to extend your hand down to someone who is reaching up for yours.

Now go out there and play some tennis!

"THE KEY IS TO KEEP COMPANY ONLY WITTH PEOPLE WHO UPLIFT YOU, WHOSE PRESENCE CALLS FORTH YOUR BEST." – EPICTETUS

CHAPTER 43

THE PROBLEM IS WE THINK WE HAVE TIME

When you're young you think you have all the time in the world. The older you get the more you realize just how much of a precious commodity it is.

Unfortunately most people fall into the trap of thinking they have all the time in the world. The truth is none of know how much time we have on this earth. Sorry to sound so morbid, but if we all lived like we were dying we'd sure as hell get a lot more done.

One of my favourite expressions is: don't get to the end and wish you had.

Do you really want to get to the end of your life and regret the decisions you didn't make, the

We all have the same amount of time in a day. The difference is how we use it.

actions you didn't take, the things you didn't say, the dreams that you kept putting aside?

If we all lived like we were running out of time or if we lived each day as if it were our last, what would we do differently? How would we act? What acts of courage would we take knowing that we have absolutely nothing to lose? Imagine what kind of life that would be.

Just breathing or alive? Most people live, but very few actually are alive. I know it sounds sad but take a moment to think about how many people sleep walk through life feeling disempowered, not feeling like they can accomplish their dreams.

I'd rather choke on greatness than nibble on mediocrity. I've always been afraid of living an average life, a life where one just goes through the motions day in and day out until one day they wake up and discover that their life has passed them by and actually could have been pretty great had they not been afraid to live it.

The problem is you can't get time back. You can use it well, waste it, but you can never get it back.

Think about how you spend your day. I always say we all have the same amount of time, the difference is in how we choose to use it. People always say to me, Maria, how the heck do you get so much done? Well, first of all I disconnected TV 4 years ago THAT frees up a lot of time. Seriously though, I know the value of my time and I treat it with respect.

CHAPTER 44

IT'S JUST A HABIT

It's never too late to change your life. You have the ability to create whatever you desire at any time. It just comes down to the CHOICES we make on a daily basis, which form our habits.

The good ones can propel us to unthinkable success.

The bad ones can destroy everything.

"GOOD HABITS ARE HARD TO FORM BUT EASY TO LIVE WITH. BAD HABITS ARE EASY TO FORM AND HARD TO LIVE WITH." – BRIAN TRACY

You always have a choice. Choose wisely. Choose differently. The results don't lie. You are where you are based on the choices you have or haven't made. We all are.

You are your choices

What you choose is who you are....

Bad choices create bad habits. Bad habits one on top of the other are the obstacles and roadblocks to your success.

A great life is made up of small seemingly insignificant choices on a daily even hourly basis that add up and contribute to a big life!

> *Good habits are hard to form but easy to live with. Bad habits are easy to form and hard to live with.*
> — BRIAN TRACY

Good choices are not easy to make. It's not easy to choose to get up an hour earlier to run instead of stay in your warm bed, or to stay at home and study while your friends are out having fun.

These choices are somewhat of a sacrifice, but nothing great comes easy.

Here's the good news, the more you make better choices, the easier it becomes. The better choices start forming into habits, and once that is done, there's no breaking those! Habits form the foundation of our lives. What we repeatedly do day in day out equals who we are.

CHAPTER 45

GO TO A PLACE OF DISCOMFORT

Go to a place of discomfort and push, and push, and push. The calming, steady voice of my yoga instructor repeated over and over encouraging us to deepen our stretch. To go a little further than we did yesterday, to lean into it a bit more, a bit longer, just enough to feel the discomfort and then release.

It was not easy, taking your body to where it's never gone before is uncomfortable. I wanted to go back to where it was comfortable. It's not easy and sure as hell not fun. But what happens is that as we ease into the discomfort it slowly starts to feel comfortable, and that's how our bodies transform.

Go to a place of discomfort until it becomes a place of comfort she repeated.

It's the same way with our minds. Our minds always want to keep us safe, to keep us comfortable. Anytime we feel awkward, scared, uneasy about something it's our minds job to pull us back to where we feel safe. But guess what? Comfort zones are where dreams go to die. Nothing exciting EVER happens in your comfort zone and frankly never will.

You must feel the discomfort to get to the place of comfort.

Everything is difficult before it's easy. We look at all the people who are successful and think wow, they must have something I don't. There must be some magic pill she swallowed and I have to find it! Trust me, there is no magic pill. The only thing you have to do is push yourself a little bit each time, more than before. This is how progress works. This is how we get ahead and change our lives, one step at a time.

And we take that step or make that move that feels uncomfortable because we know that after a while it won't feel like that anymore.

Every next level of your life will demand a different version of you, and unless you are constantly pushing yourself to a place of discomfort, you will never get there.

A comfort zone is the place where dreams go to die.

What do I mean by discomfort? I mean getting up that extra hour to go to the gym, making that extra sales call when all you want to do is give up, getting your idea out of your head and taking that first scary step, putting down the chocolate bar and reaching for fruit instead.

Nobody likes to feel uncomfortable, uncertain, scared. I assure you anyone that has ever achieved anything of greatness and anything worth talking about has experienced all of these feelings and has pushed past them to get to the other side.

What are you going to do today to feel a little uncomfortable?

You can't read the label on the outside of the jar when you're inside the jar.

#GirlWithAPlanBook

CHAPTER 46

GET OUT OF TOWN

When we are on the road to building our dream we can often feel stuck. This is normal but it can also be very frustrating and potentially lead us to quit which is not what a girl with a plan does!

Realize that on your journey to building the life you dream of you will get tired along the way and you will need to rest and that's totally acceptable. Do not be discouraged and remember to keep going.

"I may pause and rest but I will never stop."

Taking breaks is important and so is gaining a fresh and new perspective. The best way to do this is to immerse yourself in new environments and place yourself deliberately in new situations. Meet new people, go to places you've never been before.

Now you might be thinking, yes I'd love to travel but I can't afford it. First of all get rid of that phrase right away! You don't need to be a millionaire to get out of town!

Get rid of the above phrase as well as these ones:

I don't know how. Find out how, learn, and ask questions until you know how.

I don't have money. Remember that whatever we say to the universe, it always responds YES. Stop saying you don't have money and start saying, "Money flows to me easily and effortlessly from multiple sources and I am always being divinely guided."

I don't have the time. I hate this one, and unfortunately it is one of the most used excuses out there as to why people are not living their dream. You always have the time to do what is important to you and what you deem a priority.

We may say that something is a priority to us like living our dream for example, yet we don't take the actions that are in alignment with making that dream a reality. We waste our times scrolling aimlessly through Facebook instead of taking concrete steps and making a plan to fulfill our dreams. Our priorities are reflected in what we DO, not in what we say we are going to do.

You can only get results by taking action. It's that simple. Knowledge without application is useless. Action, even imperfect action is always better than doing nothing. Those that risk nothing are nothing, become nothing and have nothing.

So what do we do when we are feeling stuck and discouraged and seem to have given up hope?

Here's the plan:

Get out of town!

That's right you heard me, go to a place that you've never been before. It doesn't have to cost a lot of money, but it is important that you change your environment and do it often. Changing environments gives you a fresh new perspective, it gives you a renewed sense of self confidence and ammunition to stay in the game. It allows you to relax and see things from the outside. One of my favourite expressions is: You can't see the label on the outside of the jar when you're on the inside. Sometimes all it takes is for you to remove yourself from a certain environment or situation to allow you to see it more clearly.

You don't even have to fly. You can just get in your car and drive to somewhere you've never been before. Spend time there away from your current surroundings. Time away from your everyday hustle and bustle allows you to really focus in on what's most important to you. It gives you a sense of clarity and a fresh set of eyes. It also opens you up to new possibilities and may even provide solutions to problems you never thought of before.

When you return you will notice yourself energized and invigorated and ready to take things on with more zeal and vigor. Getting away also allows you to reflect on how far you've come and all the things that you've accomplished.

> *"THE WORLD IS A BOOK, AND THOSE THAT DO NOT TRAVEL READ ONLY ONE PAGE."*

This chapter was written from a coffee shop. I had been at home all morning writing and was feeling a bit stuck so I decided to grab my laptop and head to my neighbourhood cafe. It helped! I managed to feel inspired and finished this chapter in 30 minutes. That's what changing environments can do for you.

CHAPTER 47

DRESS FOR SUCCESS

Dress for success? Really? How shallow you might think. I don't want people to judge me based on the way I look.

I hate to break it to you but people will formulate an impression about you based on the first few seconds of meeting you. Wouldn't you want to portray what you want them to think of you?

Be picky with you friends, clothes and time.

You'll never get a second chance to make a great first impression, so why not put your best foot forward?

You might be thinking well I don't have the time to dress up or the money to spend on expensive clothes, but truth is you don't need to spend a fortune to look good and it takes just as much time to look like a slob as it does to put on a power suit.

DIVA ON A BUDGET

First of all ladies, fabulous is an attitude, not the price tag of your dress or how expensive your handbag is. If you can remember this, you won't go broke trying to look fabulous.

You've heard the expression, a man makes the clothes, the clothes do not make the man!

Fabulous shines from within. No matter what you have on.

This being said, it is important to always look your best, and at the same time to not break the bank doing it.

Possible. Doable. Just remember less is more.

Keep classic pieces in your closet. A fabulous black suit, a perfect fitting black dress, the perfect pair of pumps, and accessories, accessories, accessories.

A beautiful set of vintage pearls, a scarf that can be tied so many ways, a hat, sunglasses, an eye-catching bracelet.

And keep in mind, looking good is all about keeping in shape so that your clothes fit properly on you. You could have all the best designer clothes at your disposal but if you don't feel good about your body, nothing is going to look good on you.

Confidence. Posture. Head held high. All signs of a Girl With A Plan, and signature traits of a woman with the purpose to be fabulous, and fearless.

Why is it so important that you dress the way you want to be addressed? Because it's all about attitude and how you feel when you look good. Do you notice how your posture changes when you put on something that you feel good in? The physical changes also transmute to emotional change. We know that we attract what we feel and what we radiate. So when we feel successful and confident we will attract more success like a magnet.

When we are wearing an outfit that portrays success, we FEEL successful and so we then ACT successful and people respond to us as that. We will get more of the same. The more successful you feel, the more successful you act. The more successful you act, the more success comes your way. It can be no other way, this is the law of attraction in action.

Don't save dressing your best for a special occasion. Every day of your life is a special occasion. Wear the fancy shoes, use the good china and dress each day as if you're going to meet your worst enemy or an ex, whichever one makes you want to look your best!

The way you dress reflects how you portray yourself and how you perceive yourself and in turn how others perceive you. How we dress speaks volumes about how we take care of ourselves, it shows the world how much care we put into ourselves. Caring about yourself and your appearance spills over to other areas in life.

If you do not value yourself enough to take care of your appearance and present yourself in the best light possible, others will follow your example and they will not value you either.

Taking care of yourself shows that you have the ability to take care of others, including taking care of business.

CHAPTER 48

BEES LOVE HONEY

In life delivery is everything. The way you say something and the tone in your voice has the power to convey a thousand meanings. Through a lot of trial and error I have discovered that when it comes to asking for what you want, adding pretty please with a little sugar on top always yields more success.

Go with the wave not against it. Riding the wave is so much easier than trying to swim against it.

When my son was 2-years old, and my husband at the time walked out on us I held so much anger and resentment. I could just not get rid of. As the years passed and he became more involved in my son's life, the lines of communication opened up. They had to.

Time really does heal all wounds and there's nothing you can do to rush that. It's important that you try to take steps forward as little as they may be, but eventually it all becomes water under the bridge and the pain does gradually dissipate.

I found that when I'm asking for something it's always better to ask nicely rather than be constantly on the attack. People will always respond to how you treat them and how you make them feel. You'll have much better success at attracting bees with honey than you will with vinegar.

You can catch more flies with honey than with vinegar.

CHAPTER 49

THE LAST 5 MINUTES

Did you know that the most important 5 minutes of your day are spent in bed right before you doze off to sleep?

These 5 minutes literally have the power to change your life and help you reach your goals and dreams faster.

So here's the plan. You can try this tonight and every night until you see your dream become a reality.

Your subconscious mind is most comfortable when you are unconscious and that is when you are asleep. In your sleep state, your subconscious mind is very busy at work and will go to work realizing all the instructions that you feed it.

The last 5 minutes of your day are so important because it's this time that you lay in bed and you're feeling relaxed and getting drowsy that your subconscious is most powerful. Whatever you tell your subconscious mind will replay over and over again for the next 8 hours. Your subconscious will prepare and deliver all the instructions that you give it, so the question is, what do you want to think about and how do you want to think about it?

Most people, as they are about to enter into sleep use the last minutes of their day just before they drift off to review all of the things that went wrong that day. They think about all of the things that they are not happy about. They use this time to review all of the things that didn't work, all of the people who did them wrong or who hurt them. Essentially most people use this time for worrying.

If we think about the Law of Attraction, it is clear that when we think about or speak about what we DON'T want to happen, that is in fact what will show up in our life. What we need to do during this very powerful time is program our minds with all the things that we WANT to manifest, and not complain or worry about the things that did not.

I'm not where I want to be yet, but I am a lot closer than I was yesterday.

We attract into our lives whatever we put our attention, energy and focus on whether positive or negative, and most of this happens on a subconscious level. So why not take advantage of this time to give your subconscious the instructions that you would like it carry out?

We attract what we feel. This is really important to understand, so if we are feeling negative, sad, angry, hurt, the universe will give us more of that. If on the other hand we cultivate the feeling of love, power, influence, joy, success, then the universe also gives us more of that.

Remember that the subconscious mind is open to suggestion and will carry out the orders that it is given. What are you suggesting to it every night before you go to bed?

Stop programming your subconscious mind to review all the things you don't want, all the things that went wrong, all the things that are not working, and instead re-program it with positive affirmations, and the best way to do this is to start with the sentence: I AM.

Use the last 5 minutes of your day to fill in the blank after the I AM Statement with whatever you want to manifest into your life.

I am wealthy
I am healthy
I am wise
I am lucky
I am grateful
I am prosperous
I am happy
I am productive
I am ....

Program your mind with the things you do want.

Imagine that God is giving you a currency to purchase anything that you want, but instead you go out shopping and you purchase everything that you don't want, then you come home and have a house full of things you don't want! Sounds a little crazy doesn't it, but unfortunately this is how most people live. They keep focusing on what they don't want and then wonder why they never get what they do want.

The currency that you have for attracting what it is you DO want into your life are your words which lead to your thoughts which lead to your feelings and emotions which lead to your results.

Anything that you want to attract, be, do or have in your life begins with what you have placed in your imagination and the words you are putting after I AM. Whatever we place after the I AM we are inviting into our life. Make sure you are sealing your intentions with the right instructions.

Repetition is the key to success and programming your subconscious takes time. Do this every night before you sleep, doing it once and then falling back to your old ways is not going to give you any result.

Try asking yourself this question every night before you drift off...how would I be feeling right now if all my dreams and wishes were a reality? It's this feeling that you want to concentrate on as you drift off to sleep.

CHAPTER 50

IT ALL ADDS UP

Patience is one of the key factors to success. Without it nothing is possible. Without it we cannot endure or withstand the obstacles and the struggles that every entrepreneur's journey will sure be filled with.

What is a great life? It's actually just a series of small steps taken on a daily basis. These small steps add up to a big life.

It's the small, seemingly insignificant things that you do on a minute to minute basis, on an hourly basis and on a daily basis that cause the long-term results.

Often times when we are trying to reach a goal we feel like we're NEVER going to get there. Such has been my experience particularly because I'm a high achieving type A personality. But, this is the wrong attitude and mindset to be in.

We have to realize that Rome was not built in a day and that great things take time. I always like to say some progress is better than none, and I may not be where I want to be today but I sure as hell am a lot further than I was yesterday.

If you are taking action every single day and doing something, anything that will move you in the direction of your goal, you will get there.

Anyone that keeps putting one foot at a time in front of the other will surely arrive at her destination. It may not be in the time that you want to, but it will be in the time that is right for you.

Every experience that you have is leading you to the place where you will eventually end up. Every experience is necessary to have to get you to the next one. There is always a reason why you are still where you are. Maybe it's a lesson you still need to learn, maybe it's because you don't have the foundations in place for the growth that you want at this moment, maybe God is giving you more time to prepare, to get ready, to be the person you need to be in order to receive what is coming your way.

You must live in faith and know that everything you are doing today IS making a difference for tomorrow even though at times it may not feel like it.

Sometimes I work out for days at a time and I get frustrated because I still don't see the pounds drop and I become incredibly impatient, but then all of a sudden when I least expect it, out of nowhere the pounds suddenly drop.

The work you're putting in today IS making a difference for the results that are coming in your future.

Some days it may just feel like a drop in the bucket, but know that those drops eventually fill the bucket.

Success is a deliberate set of actions taken on a consistent basis.

CHAPTER 51

DON'T TAKE THE NEXT FLIGHT OUT

On the road less traveled to success you will be tempted to take the next flight out. I promise you there will be countless times that you'll feel like giving up on your dreams, and packing it all in and returning to the same comfortable feeling of home.

You didn't come this far, to only come this far.

Don't be that person. Don't be the one who makes it so far only to turn back when things get tough, and I promise you, they will get tough.

Do you know what most people do when things get overwhelming, and they become frustrated with the progress or lack thereof? You guessed it! They give up. It is often said that when we are close to reaching our goal that this will be the time that we want to give up. Don't quit before the miracle happens. Don't quit because you believe you'll never get there. What happens to quitters? Nothing. They never get to where they want to go because they stop trying.

I wonder what will happen if I don't give up.

Do you want to know how to become unstoppable? Move past the places that you would normally stop. Sounds simple, but definitely not easy.

The path to success is not a straight and narrow one, as most people seem to think. It's paved with disappointments, failures, learning experiences, mistakes and hardships. These are all there to make us stronger, to make us more resilient, to test us to see if we want it bad enough.

Supporters to prove right and doubters to prove wrong!

It's often the last key in the bunch that opens the door. So with that being said, don't be discouraged if the first key doesn't open the lock. It's not supposed to. You need to keep trying all the keys, until eventually the right one opens the door.

People look at the success of others and they will immediately do one of two things. They will start to compare themselves to the successful person and lose faith and become discouraged at how much further they have to go to catch up. Beware of comparing your success to others. Everyone is on a different path and moves along at a different speed, and I assure you the success of others has taken time to build and it did not happen overnight.

Stop comparing your behind the scenes to everyone else's production reel.

This is definitely a recipe for disaster and will impede and stunt your growth. Look to others for inspiration and encouragement and proof that yes, it CAN be done, and believe that one day you will get there too.

CHAPTER 52

KEEP IT MOVING SISTER!

Keep moving forward even if all you can see is five feet ahead of you. Action in the direction of your dreams is imperative. Consistent action must be taken daily. Most of us stall because we are not sure how our big dream is going to unfold or how it's all going to work. The thing is, you don't need to know that, nor will you have to.

If you can't run then walk, if you can't walk, then crawl.

"EVEN A SNAIL WILL EVENTUALLY REACH IT'S DESTINATION" – GAIL TSUKIYAMA

You just need these two things: the courage to take action and the courage to keep going and persisting even when you don't see the results....

If you can develop these two skills you will excel at being an entrepreneur.

Do it even when you don't feel like doing it. All successful people are self-motivated, that means that they push themselves to accomplish the things that need accomplishing even when they don't feel like it!

Anyone can get things done when they're in the mood, it's what happens when you aren't in the mood or the motivation is just not there. These are the moments that winners push through.

"SUCCESS CONSISTS OF GOING FROM FAILURE TO FAILURE WITHOUT LOSS OF ENTHUSIASM"- WINSTON CHURCHILL

Persist until you succeed. Always take another step, even when you're tired. Then take another, and yet another. In truth, one step at a time is not too difficult. I know that small attempts, repeated, will get you to where you want to go.

"TAKE THE FIRST STEP IN FAITH. YOU DON'T HAVE TO SEE THE WHOLE STAIRCASE. JUST TAKE THE FIRST STEP." - MARTIN LUTHER KING JR.

Remember what makes a big life. The succession of small steps strung together until they add up to that giant leap that everyone thinks happened overnight.

Longfellow once wrote: "Those heights by great men, won and kept, were not achieved by sudden flight. But they, while their companions slept, were toiling upward in the night."

You can accomplish anything you want if only you give up the belief that you can't. Keep putting one foot in front of the other and dream with your eyes wide open.

I believe in you.

With love.

You didn't come this far only to come this far.

CORE VALUES LIST

Below is a list of core values commonly used. This list is not exhaustive, but it will give you an idea of some common core values (also called personal values). My recommendation is to select five core values to focus on—if everything is a core value, then nothing is really a priority.

Authenticity	Fame
Achievement	Friendships
Adventure	Fun
Authority	Growth
Autonomy	Happiness
Balance	Honesty
Beauty	Humor
Boldness	Influence
Compassion	Inner
Challenge	Harmony
Citizenship	Justice
Community	Kindness
Competency	Knowledge
Contribution	Leadership
Creativity	Learning
Curiosity	Love
Determination	Loyalty
Fairness	Meaningful
Faith	Work

Openness	Self-Respect
Optimism	Service
Passion	Spirituality
Peace	Stability
Pleasure	Success
Poise	Status
Popularity	Trustworthiness
Recognition	Wealth
Reputation	Wisdom
Respect	
Responsibility	
Security	

ADDITIONAL RESOURCES

TAKE YOUR SUCCESS TO THE NEXT LEVEL....

To learn more about the Ladies WHO Lunch® Network and how you can benefit from being a member of this global community visit www.LWLNetwork.com to claim your exclusive invite to join today!

WORK WITH MARIA:

Idea To Reality - a guide to using the Law of Attraction to get anything you want in life.
Visit www.IdeaToRealityCourse.com

She's in Biz Blueprint - an online course "Helping Female Entrepreneurs Turn Their Passion into a Profitable Business" visit www.ShesInBizBlueprint.com

WWW.GIRLWITHAPLANBOOK.COM

ABOUT THE AUTHOR

Maria is a multi-passionate entrepreneur who went from teaching high school to starting her own international school at the age of twenty eight and later going on to launch a Teacher Training Centre. Maria's sociable nature and business savvy led her to a successful career selling real estate in Vancouver. As a single mom, her true passion lies in connecting and inspiring women to realize that anything is possible for themselves.

She is the founder of the Ladies WHO Lunch ® Network and creator of the She's in Biz Blueprint, who believes that surrounding yourself with like-minded, positive and inspirational individuals is the most successful formula for creating and manifesting your dreams. Her mission is to inspire women to be fearless and fabulous by helping them realize and live their dream.

#GirlWithAPlanBook

www.ingramcontent.com/pod-product-compliance
Lightning Source LLC
Chambersburg PA
CBHW020904080526
44589CB00011B/430